THE STIGMATIZED CHILD

"Mommy, am I stupid?"
Helping Parents Overcome the Stigma attached to
Learning Disabilities, ADHD, and Lack of Social Skills

Other Books
by
Anne Ford and John-Richard Thompson

Laughing Allegra: The Inspiring Story of a Mother's Struggle and Triumph Raising a Daughter with Learning Disabilities

On Their Own: Creating an Independent Future for Your Adult Child with Learning Disabilities and ADHD

A Special Mother: Getting Through the Early Days of a Child's Diagnosis of Learning Disabilities and Related Disorders

The Forgotten Child: "If She is Special, What am I?" Sibling Issues: When Learning Disabilities Cause Tension in the Home

INTRODUCTION

One morning, very early, a little after 5:30 a.m., a mother hustled her young son into a taxi and began their daily ride to lower Manhattan. All during the school year they made the same journey at the same early hour, day after day, month after month. This mother's parents knew nothing about it. Her wide circle of friends had no clue, nor did her sister or brother-in-law: no one but her husband knew about the early morning taxis.

It sounds like the beginning of a spy novel, doesn't it? What could be the cause of such secrecy? Was her son meeting with a CIA agent? Was he involved with an underground criminal organization?

No.

He was meeting with a tutor to get extra help because he had learning disabilities.

The boy's mother told me this story after her son had graduated from high school and the secret morning tutors were long in the past, and I consider it a fine illustration of a wrong way to deal with (or rather *not* deal with) the stigma associated with learning disabilities.

The dictionary defines *stigma* as "a mark of shame or discredit; a stain or reproach, as on one's reputation," and "a set of negative and often unfair beliefs that a society or group of people have about something." The word *stigma* originally indicated a mark or a brand used to identify a slave in ancient days. Merriam-Webster tells us that once the word passed into the English language it became associated with a mark or stain you cannot always see and so today we hear about

1

the stigma of homelessness, the stigma of obesity, and the stigma of mental illness. People may be so afraid of being stigmatized due to unemployment that they'll put on their office clothes and drive out their driveways every weekday morning so that the neighbors won't know. That same fear could convince a parent to drive the lonely roads before the sun came up to avoid letting anyone know her son was seeing a tutor.

Few parents would use the words "shame or discredit; a stain or reproach" when describing their child's learning disabilities or their efforts to hide those disabilities. At the same time, many parents and children believe those words exactly describe how society views a learning disability or related disorder. Some have had first-hand experience with their child (or themselves) being treated as a person with a shameful condition.

Dr. Jeffrey Lieberman in his book *Shrinks: The Untold Story of Psychiatry* talks of the stigma associated with mental illness. "It is still regarded as a mark of shame," he says, "a scarlet letter C for 'crazy,' P for 'psycho,' or M for 'mental.' Imagine you were invited to a friend's wedding but unexpectedly came down with an illness. Would you prefer to say that you had to cancel because of a kidney stone…or a manic episode?"

The same can be said for learning disabilities and the ways we view them. Let's say you are an adult with severe dyslexia and you are unexpectedly asked to read something aloud on a blackboard at a company meeting. Would you rather say you were having trouble seeing because you forgot your glasses….or because you have a reading disability? If you have ADHD, would you rather tell a friend the subway was delayed…or that you were so distracted you completely forgot the time and place where you were supposed to meet?

There are so many layers to the problem of stigma. Some parents, hoping to avoid "labeling" their child, can actually contribute to the child's sense of stigma. Secretive behavior can lead a child to believe he or she has something to be ashamed of. *Don't tell anyone. No one needs to know.* No one expresses these sentiments over things they feel positive about. Some parents are unaffected or unaware or – best of all - unconcerned about what others think, even as their own child does all he or she can to keep the LD a secret. Other parents suffer through agonies over what others think or say about their child (or their own parenting abilities), while the child blithely skips through life without a care in the world.

I have found that a parent's sense of stigma is most acute when the child is newly diagnosed (or a little before). This is the time when many parents do all they can to avoid labeling the child. In some cases, and up to a certain point, this is understandable. A child diagnosed with mild dyslexia probably doesn't need the whole Special Education label, but a child who unquestionably *needs* Special Ed is granted no favors when a parent delays treatment or avoids it altogether due to fears of a label.

For young adults, the stigma often comes late in high school and into the college years. I can't tell you how many times I have heard that someone has dropped out of college (or flunked out) because they refused to acknowledge their disability and seek the help that is readily available at nearly every college in the United States.

Why are these parents and children so reluctant to acknowledge something that so obviously affects so much of their lives? Those very same parents would have no trouble acknowledging a physical disability, no more than a child in a wheelchair would make an effort to hide it.

The reason is obvious and intractable, and it is wholly to do with societal realities. There is a large and stubborn strain within the population at large that refuses to include LD in the list of "acceptable" conditions and persists in believing learning disabilities and related disorders are simply excuses for laziness or poor parenting. There is no question that more acceptance and less skepticism by the general public would help many more parents get past the hurdle of the infamous *Label*.

When I served as Chairman of the National Center for Learning Disabilities, we commissioned a Roper Poll about public attitudes about learning disabilities. Here is a result of their findings under the heading: *Stigma*

There continues to be a stigma associated with learning disabilities for most people – perhaps stemming from a lack of understanding about learning disabilities. Signs of this stigma emerge in both explicit and implicit ways.

•   *About half of the General Public and Parents agree that learning disabilities are often just laziness.*

• *A majority of the General Public and Parents believe that learning disabilities are often a product of the home environment children are raised in. Four in ten teachers and three in ten administrators also agree*

The report went on to say, *These types of misunderstandings about learning disabilities being laziness or being caused by a home environment are not conducive to parents being open to early diagnosis and intervention for learning disabilities. Nor does it bode well for Educators seeing Parents as partners in addressing the issues. Thus it is perhaps not surprising that four in ten parents believe that "other parents" would opt to address their children's learning disabilities privately, rather than turning to teachers.*

These findings illustrate the prominent role of stigma when early diagnosis and intervention is delayed. The perceived stigma of LD persuades many parents to continue to ignore potential signs of trouble. Instead, they choose to wait and see if their child will "grow out of it".

Many parents will continue with the wait and see attitude long after they have already waited too long and seen ample evidence that there is a problem. Examples abound when it comes to the specific issue of medication for ADHD (which is not LD, but is a related disorder and is often found in those who have LD). Some parents have a deep-seated opposition to giving the medication to their child. This might be understandable until we ask if they would hesitate in quite the same way to provide medication if the child was born with a physical illness such as a heart problem. (This is not to say there are not other treatments or approaches for ADHD that can be effective, only that some parents outright refuse to consider medication the moment it is suggested.)

In one such case I know, a mother in Florida absolutely refuses to put her child on medication for his rather severe ADHD. She has tried every other intervention known, from occupational therapy to some highly suspect ones such as brain scans. None of them have made a bit of difference and therefore the boy continues to run an endless gauntlet of ridicule and disapproval for his inability to pay attention or focus on even the simplest tasks. After his diagnosis of ADHD, he received extra time on his exams, which, in turn, caused more than a few negative comments from his classmates and their parents. It is possible he would continue to need extra time on his exams even if he did take the medication but no one really knows since that treatment has never been tried. This boy's parents are adding to his sense of being stigmatized by allowing him to go through all the difficulties associated with ADHD, even though there may be a proven way to alleviate those same difficulties.

Let's look at another, similar situation involving a nine year old girl also diagnosed with ADHD (coincidentally also in Florida). This mother, too, was reluctant to use any type of medication unless absolutely necessary – but for her, the pediatrician was able to convince her that the medication was, indeed, "absolutely necessary." The first day her daughter took the drug, the usual chaos at the dinner table vanished. This was not the girl her parents knew. Usually, she was up and down from the table, causing a commotion. At school she had a great deal of trouble concentrating or paying attention to anything, but her grades suddenly improved and her circle of friendships widened.

I am obviously an advocate of trying any treatment that has been proven to be safe and effective. Having said that, there are also many false "treatments" out there, and charlatans just waiting to raise parent's hopes with unsound and unproven therapies. I made a mistake thirty years ago (and I know another mother who is doing the same thing now) when I drove my daughter Allegra out to Long Island and had a doctor run water into her ears because he was convinced her challenges were due to an inner ear problem.

He prescribed Compazine, a medication used for sea sickness, but it none of it worked. Other treatments such as spinning, in my opinion, fall into the category of "questionable practices".

One of the peculiar aspects of learning disabilities and related disorders is that most efforts to hide it make it come into the light.

In my book *A Special Mother*, one of the mothers, Janie, pointed this out to her husband when he voiced a concern about acknowledging his son's LD. "My husband was really concerned about the label," Janie said. "He wondered aloud, 'What are people going to say?' Eventually I told him, "It doesn't matter what people say because they'll be saying a lot worse things if we don't get him some help and he isn't able to finish school."

One of the greatest – possibly *the* greatest contributing factor to stigma, to being bullied or ostracized from the group is social skills, or rather, a lack of social skills. It looms so large that I will go into it in detail in this book. I believe social skills are the most important factor in a child's happiness. Academics are important, of course, but if you know your multiplication tables but have no idea how to carry on a conversation, you will face all sorts of unexpected difficulties. Positive social skills can cover so many flaws. Poor social skills can exacerbate them.

I know a young man with LD who seems unable to converse about anything that does not involve Nascar racing. He is a handsome, capable young man, but in every conversation he talks about racing in a droning voice, on and on, with no sense of when to stop. Because of his LD, he is unable to read visual cues and cannot see when people are getting bored. As a result, even the nicest, most patient people try to avoid having a conversation with him unless absolutely necessary. I am a very big advocate of finding your child's strengths and interests and pushing them: in this case (admittedly extreme), his interest has overwhelmed all other aspects of life to such an extent that they have created new problems. The stigma brought on by a lack of social skills can lead to isolation, a lack of friends, and conflict.

My own daughter Allegra has few troubles with social skills (thankfully). I will go into her story in detail in the next chapter, but I'd like to give an example of how LD and some challenges with social skills caused a problem in her life. I've heard other mothers tell of similar incidents, so I do not believe it is uncommon. When my daughter was about twelve, she was playing the board game Chutes and Ladders with two much younger children. As most mothers know, Chutes and Ladders is extremely popular and requires very little in the way of mathematical skills. You spin a spinner and move the number of spaces indicated by where the spinner stops, but for someone with learning disabilities, even the most minimal abilities required to play the game may be out of reach. Allegra could not move the pieces where they were supposed to go. If she was supposed to move the piece forward, she moved it back. If she was supposed to move the piece two spaces, she moved it five, or one, or whichever felt right to her. The younger children couldn't comprehend the possibility that a "big kid" couldn't play a game they so easily understood and so they resorted to the only possibility that made any sense: she was cheating. Of course, she wasn't. Cheating was the last thing on her mind, and to be honest, I'm not sure she could figure out how to cheat. None of that mattered at the time. After a round of accusations of cheating and heated denials, the two younger ones hit upon an answer: they would never again ask her to play a board game with them.

That answer is so often the one children hit upon when it comes to a classmate with LD. Just stop playing with them.

Sometimes this is done out of confusion, as it was with the Chutes and Ladders board game ("Why can't she figure this out?") Sometimes it is done out of malice. Whichever it is, the result is often the same: loneliness, confusion, isolation and a lingering, oppressive sense of inadequacy.

In this book, we will explore the various ways stigma can enter the lives of children and adults with LD and related disorders. We will also look at ways stigma affects the parents (you may not think it does affect us parents, but trust me, it can enter into our lives in ways as damaging as the stigma faced by our children.)

I cannot pretend that a single book can change the way society views those with LD. We have all heard the expression that children can be cruel. It is a common expression for a reason. Children *can* be cruel; they can be mean; they can have a complete lack of empathy. So can adults. Like most sane, rational beings, I have a fervent hope that this will one day change. Because I am sane and rational, I also realize that hope is not likely to come to pass for quite some time. We need to accept that these cruelties exist in the world. We must confront them and stamp them out when we can – and figure ways to get beyond them when we cannot. It is impossible to eradicate them completely as they are based, in part, on fears and misunderstandings that are not easily assuaged. I believe the general public is coming around on some types of LD and related disorders. Dyslexia and ADHD, for instance, are not considered taboo subjects (though I've found that the people who most readily joke about "my dyslexia" or "having an ADHD moment" are those who have mild versions of these conditions. Those whose lives are turned upside-down by more severe dyslexia or ADHD tend to be a little more reticent.)

A more realistic hope is that we might be able to help parents overcome their own sense of stigma and to find ways to help their child get past the hurtful, negative effects brought on by LD. Such efforts can benefit us all, even those who do not have a child with disabilities in their lives.

As Dr. Jeffrey Lieberman says:

Stigma is Shame…
Shame causes Silence…
Silence hurts us all.

Let us once and for all end the silence, but let us do it in practical, useful ways. Let us shine some light on the suffering of those with any sort of disability and help them discover their place in a world that may not always understand them, but will hopefully one day come to accept and even celebrate their unique abilities.

.

Mommy Glasses

~ My Daugher Allegra ~

When we think of the stigma involved with a disability of any kind, we immediately think of the experience of the disabled person, as we should. No one faces the slings and arrows of stigma in quite the same way, and those of us who do not have a disability can only imagine what it must be like to face ridicule and misunderstandings on a daily basis. If we pull back from that image of stigma, we begin to see it can take other forms and affect other people in ways we might not immediately expect.

Some who have more severe learning disabilities may face stigma but may also be unaware of it. I cannot say without reservation that this is a blessing (though I suspect it is), and I do not have to look very far to see it.

My daughter Allegra falls into this category. Yes, she has faced stigma and I have often wondered if she has been adversely affected by it, but overall, she has had the good fortune to both not notice and not care.

After I wrote my first book *Laughing Allegra*, a memoir about raising my daughter, she would sometimes refer to herself as "someone who *used to have* learning disabilities." When writing that same book, the principal at one of her former schools told me that Allegra probably didn't remember that she had few friends when she was growing up. She would take on some of her brother Alessandro's memories, the principal told me, and since Alessandro had many friends, she would remember that she did too. I'm not sure I buy this. In fact, I'm quite sure I don't. I believe Allegra, unlike so many of us, simply has an ability to block out unpleasant things from the past and create better memories in their place; but whether she truly has forgotten what it was like in those early difficult years or if she has refashioned them into other, more tolerable memories, I would say her relationship to stigma is not a close one.

Stigma has not hovered over her. It has not followed her. It has not affected her life in overtly negative ways. Her social skills were always better than most and have turned out to be among the most positive aspects of her life. There were a few little bumps in the road along the way, but for the most part, I will say my daughter was lucky enough to be spared the ravages of stigma experienced by so many others.

And her mother? Not so lucky.

When I speak of stigma, or think of stigma, the reality is that it nearly always centers near or upon me and my own attitudes toward my daughter's disabilities. Even when I think back to an episode that clearly affected Allegra, I cannot separate her genuine experience from my perceptions of that same experience. If a child snubbed her, or ignored her, that event truly did happen. No one made it up. If Allegra noticed it or was hurt by it, chances are she would long ago have gotten over it or completely forgotten it. But me? Oh no. I haven't forgotten. I haven't gotten over it. I remember the most insignificant little slight or insult to my daughter as if it happened this morning, even if it happened over forty years ago.

If I said to Allegra, "Remember that time the girls went by in the golf cart?" and left it at that, she would look at me as if I was insane and say, "What girls? What golf cart? What are you talking about?" But I only need to hear the words "girls" and "golf cart" in the same sentence and I am brought back to a family vacation in Nassau. Lots of our family friends were there with their children who were the same ages as my children. I went to the pool every day and Allegra joined me, not because she wanted to but because none of the other girls would include her. I can so vividly remember one specific moment at the pool, when some of the girls came by in a golf cart and waved to her and called out "Hi Allegra" in what I heard as a taunting way, and making it more than clear they weren't about to stop and ask her to join them. This was outright bullying for no apparent reason. Allegra handled it as best she could.

She had a book with her. *The Diary of Anne Frank.* She pretended to be so absorbed in the book that she didn't notice her "friends" passing by, but I knew she was pretending because when I glanced at the book, I saw she was holding it upside-down.

Let me take you back to the beginning of my story with LD, with a focus on my reactions to stigma, both real and perceived. To start, I had no notions of stigma at all for I had no expectations that learning disabilities would enter our lives. Even after LD did appear, I still did not fully understand the implications. A friend of mine has an expression: "mommy glasses," meaning the inability to see a problem when it stares you in the face. All mothers wear them to some extent. We see the good and the positive in our child. We put on our mommy glasses and problems melt away or become so small we no longer notice them.

I had prescription-strength mommy glasses and it took a long, long time for me to take them off. When I did, I saw far more than I wanted to see, and even a few things that were not there.

This is how it happened.

My daughter was born before some of you mothers reading this book were born: on January 3, 1972. There were no serious difficulties with her birth and no unusual problems during her infancy. Her brother Alessandro was seven at the time she was born, and I fully expected and believed I had two perfectly fine, happy, healthy children.

That firm belief remained throughout the first years of Allegra's life. I saw no trouble on the horizon. I detected no signs of anything out of the ordinary. If I did, I was unable to see them as anything that might be associated with a "disability". Unusual behavior was always and firmly attributed to developmental delays (and I didn't even think in those particular terms. When Allegra had a little trouble feeding herself and it was pointed out to me, I saw this entirely as a result of being too indulgent and not asking enough of her, and so I spent the time required to be sure she *could* feed herself. It would never have occurred to me to think of it as a sign of something wrong.)

We had about five years of a perfectly normal, blissful existence, and then suddenly, within the course of a few months, everything changed. Assumptions I had were overturned. My own expectations were forced into different, unfamiliar paths. Fear and confusion took over. Most painful of all, stigma entered my life for the first time.

We used to spend our summers on Long Island where my children could roam free and play with their neighborhood friends. Alessandro had more friends than I could count. Allegra was only five, so she didn't have the sort of close bonds that come with a little more age – though they *would* come, I had no reason to doubt it. Like all my friends with children her age, I enrolled her in a summer gymnastics class that also focused on swimming and tennis. One day I received a call from the gymnastics coach. He told me Allegra was having a little trouble keeping up with the others in her class and she seemed to have some problems following directions. I was a little surprised he would call me about something like this. She was only five, after all. "Oh, no, she's fine," I said. "She'll catch up."

"But she doesn't seem to be able to tell the difference between right and left."

"Trust, me, she'll be fine."

Children much older than Allegra had similar troubles, I reasoned. And left and right? What child didn't have trouble with that now and then? I didn't realize it at the time, but I was polishing my mommy glasses in preparation for putting them on for the first time.

Soon after that first call, I received a similar one from the swimming coach, and another from the tennis coach. They were all polite, they all tried to be as diplomatic as possible, but each one also expressed a similar concern that Allegra wasn't able to keep up with others her age. When one coach calls, it is easy to dismiss those concerns. When three do, it's time to look into it.

I decided to work with Allegra myself. I ran with her. I tumbled with her and did somersaults. We splashed around in the pool together every day. I worked with her on every gymnastics, swimming and tennis activity and found she could do them all with no problem. She even could tell her right from her left...sometimes. I sent her back to the classes, confident in her abilities to do all she was asked, and almost immediately the calls came again, telling me she could not do what I had just seen for my self that she obviously *could* do.

"She'll be fine," I told them, a little exasperated. "She'll catch up."

Near the end of the summer, there was an awards ceremony with a gymnastics exhibition and swimming competition. In spite of the coaches' assertions, it never occurred to me to keep her out. To do so would be far more damaging to her self-esteem. That's what I thought. And if she couldn't do a perfect somersault, so what? No one with any kind of sense would fault her for that.

It was a beautiful summer day and I arrived at the event wearing my most gorgeous floppy-brimmed summer hat and sunglasses. I took my seat, fully expecting Allegra to hold her own in

The lights went down on the audience and came up on the stage. It took me a little while to spot her. They began to sing, and that's when it happened. Almost immediately, all my denial, all my illusions, and all my repeated reassurances that she would catch up fell away, as if a spotlight had been cast upon them to force me to face reality.

The children were grouped together with the music teacher conducting with her back to the audience. The first song started and suddenly I saw Allegra step out in front of the other children to dance and sing a song that had absolutely nothing to do with what the others were singing. It was over in a matter of seconds. The music teacher caught her and led her back to the others, but, for me, those seconds lasted for hours, and now - for years. I can still see her there, singing something known only to her, lost, bewildered, and unable to fit in with the others. I can guarantee that no one around me noticed or, if they did, they didn't think twice about it. They might have smiled, thinking it was cute. I would have thought it was funny and cute a few months before, but now I could not escape the reality that everything the coaches and teachers told me was true.

Something truly was going on with my daughter.

The nursery school was high in a building on Madison Avenue. When I finally went to the headmistress to discuss my options, she said, "You might want to visit the school downstairs on the third floor. They have experience with children like Allegra. It's called Gateway. I think it would be a better fit for her."

I couldn't argue with that. Surely she knew what was best. I thought maybe it would be a school with fewer children per class, or more experienced teachers. I rode the elevator down and the doors opened upon a single large room (it was originally intended as a gymnasium) with small make-shift offices built around the perimeter. In the middle of the floor were the students, and to me they all appeared to be seriously disabled; some with physical disabilities, some with intellectual disabilities; some with both. I was shocked that anyone could imagine this place would be a "better fit" for Allegra.

I think that's the moment when the reality of what I was facing came crashing down upon me. The gymnastics event started it, the Christmas concert heightened it, but seeing the children at the Gateway school and the extent of their disabilities brought it all into sharp focus. There was something *wrong* with my daughter. I might not have seen it, but professionals and experts, coaches and teachers did. They saw it clearly.

I still had a few weeks of denial left in me, but events came racing forward during those months. Tests, More tests. Evaluations. None of them were conclusive, or gave me anything firm to go on. I did not know what actions to take, or how to begin tackling this problem. And then came the moment I have written about in every one of my books, and talk about in every one of my speeches, and still haunts me to this day.

If Allegra needed all these tests, I reasoned, why not take the bull by the horns and get her tested by the very best person I could find. I did some research and made an appointment with the top pediatric neurologist in New York City. He agreed to evaluate Allegra and took her into his office. I was not allowed to accompany her as he wanted to evaluate her without my influence. After it was all over, he called me into his office where he sat at a polished desk, with a rather solemn expression on his face. In a cold, disinterested voice he said, "Your daughter is mentally retarded and I feel the best thing for you, for her, and your family, is to institutionalize her. I know of an ideal place for her. It's located a few miles outside of London." Before I could respond, before I could even think of a single thing to say, he added: "And I wish I could help you with this, but I'm too busy at the moment."

This was stigma in action. This was stigma at its cruelest. At the very moment he was making his pronouncement, Allegra was outside his office at the receptionist's desk, sitting in her chair and making the receptionist laugh by pretending to answer the phone. This happy, cheerful little child was the person he said should be institutionalized. Why? Even if she had been mentally retarded, again I ask – *why?*

My guess is that he thought that raising a child such as my daughter was an inconvenience, an embarrassment, and surely I would want to do something about it. Surely I would leap at the chance to escape this burden. Surely I would not want to go through life dealing with such difficulties as my child's inability to read or do homework. Better to put her away in a safe place three-thousand miles away, out of sight, out of mind.

I refused to accept his recommendation, of course, and even now, all these years later, my blood still boils when I think of it. (I know another family who received the same recommendation from the same doctor. Like me, they did not follow his advice and their daughter eventually went on to attend Sarah Lawrence College and, later, began an internship at the National Center for Learning Disabilities where she did a superb job. I wonder, at times, how many did follow his advice, and how many families were broken up as a result.)

A short time later Allegra was definitively diagnosed with severe, multiple learning disabilities. It was not as dire as the neurologist's pronouncement, but it was devastating all the same, and would come to affect nearly every aspect of her life.

The title of this book includes Social Skills. As far as I'm concerned, a lack of social skills is the primary cause of stigma. If you can't read after your school years are over, most people will have no idea that you have this problem; but if you can't carry on a conversation without standing too close to the other person, continually saying inappropriate things, or misinterpreting everything the other person says, there could be trouble ahead. If you know your multiplication tables but can't say "hello", which do you think will cause more problems?

It is interesting to note the way we think of our children before and after a diagnosis of LD. Before Allegra's diagnosis, I viewed anything that could be considered a challenge with social skills as something normal, maybe a little puzzling, but nothing to be concerned about. She had some trouble interacting with other children. Sometimes she would be off on her own, doing her own thing, while the others were gathered around a teacher to listen to a story, or watch a movie. I noticed it, but again, it did not cause much concern at all.

After the diagnosis everything caused concern. For me, every little mistake, every misplaced word became a clear sign of her disability, even when it wasn't a sign of that at all. She might say something I thought was out of place, or a bit strange, and I would cringe. Meanwhile everyone else around us would not have noticed. If they did, they might have thought it was funny.

I carried my sense of stigma around with me all the time. I never told my friends or even close family members that Allegra was going to a special school. When someone would ask where she went to school, I would mumble something about "Gateway" and before they could ask what school it was and where it was, I would change the subject. My own mother never knew the name of the school Allegra was attending until she came to the graduation ceremony.

This was a long, painful, ridiculous effort on my part to deny the obvious. It was an inability to accept reality, as if my silence would somehow magically transform my daughter from a happy, charming, smiling girl who happened to have learning disabilities into...what? One of those perfect girls who do not have the sensitivity to include a classmate with LD in their group?

Allegra and her LD are so tied together now, and such a part of my life, and so accepted in my thoughts, that I cannot even remember what I had "hoped" for.

Her social skills took a big leap forward in an unexpected way. She received a book for Christmas when she was about seven years old called *A Very Young Skater*. It was a picture book and she fell in love with the pictures of the little Katherine Healy wearing her skating costumes. I was friends at the time with the governor of New York, Hugh Carey, and he he suggested Allegra might like to try figure skating. I did not agree. By then we had already gone through the gymnastics, tennis, swimming, and dance classes, and each one ended with the "she can't keep up," phone call. I fully expected the same with skating. She would fall, she would be unable to follow directions, she would become lost and confused, the same as she had with all the other sports and activities she tried.

I told Governor Carey my concerns and he said some of the wisest words I have ever heard: "Never give up on her," he said. "Never give failure too much power. Never doubt that your child will somehow find her way, in ways you never expect."

With reluctance, I decided to let her try. I wish I had a picture of her first step onto the ice. I stood at the side of the tiny rink, studying with amazement her joyful expression, her comfort and sense of place.

It became her passion. It became her identity. In some ways, it became her ticket out of the confusing and hurtful world of stigma. She continued to skate and in her world of skating they didn't care if she had LD or not. She still couldn't tell her right from her left, and that never changed. Even when she was older, I would write L and R on her fingertips, and once again, no one cared.

Skating gave her a sense of independence and improved her self-esteem. It gave her confidence that she could do something many of her contemporaries could not, and opened up a new world of friendships for her. She had absolutely no fear when going out before hundreds of people and performing.

Allegra attended Gateway through her grammar school years. When it came time to go to high school, I could not find any school in New York City that would accept her. This was always the case with Allegra. We had a terrible time finding a school, and each time we did, she was always accepted on a conditional basis. I never understood it. I *still* don't understand it.

Every school she attended started with this warning: "We will take her for a year, but if it doesn't work out, you'll have to find another school." This happened from kindergarten all the way up through college at Leslie University.

You can imagine why I was perplexed. I never applied to a mainstream school – only schools for children with LD. Allegra never had behavior problems. She's hardly ever had a bad mood, never mind a tantrum. How could it be a school devoted to children with similar to hers could put so many obstacles in her path?

I'm happy to say she never once was asked to leave a school. She went through every conditional period with flying colors and was off to her next challenge.

She ended up going to Riverview School in Cape Cod, Massachusetts for her high school years. Sending her there was the most difficult thing I've ever had to do. I'd never been away from her for a single night. The day I dropped her off was traumatic – for everyone. I imagine there are still dark whispers among the school staff about "about that hysterical woman".

Letting go was the supreme challenge for me, and my greatest gift to my daughter. I don't know if she ever would have gained a sense of independence and confidence had I done what I so fervently wanted; which was to keep her with me always and never let her out of sight.

I taught her to self-advocate, and eventually, when she was thirteen, she was able to fly on her own from New York to the Riverview School. This was before 9/11, so I was able to walk her right to the gate. I went over with her how she should relate to the flight attendant at the desk, and to say that she had a learning disability and needed to be helped on and off the plane. I was terrified she might be embarrassed by all of this but, in fact, she was happy to let them know she needed help. This was just the beginning of learning how to advocate for herself.

21

This newfound skill came into its own when she was returning from a trip to Orlando, Florida. She was all alone and the plane had to stop in Cincinnati due to a blizzard. Allegra called me and we went through what would happen if her plane got delayed. Three times they went to the end of the runway and three times they had to return. They finally cancelled the flight. She was able now to go to the gate desk and told the man who was on duty that she was learning disabled and had no idea what to do. We talked many times on the phone and, finally, the flight attendant was able to find a woman who was physically disabled traveling with three of her children. The woman very nicely took Allegra under her wing. They were able to find one room to accommodate all of them, including the children. The next day, the weather had cleared and they were on their way home. I spoke to the woman and thanked her profusely, and to this day, Allegra has remained friends with her.

After leaving Riverview, Allegra attended the Threshold Program at Lesley University in Cambridge, Massachusetts. This was a three-year program that focused on job-training and life skills.

After she graduated from Threshold, I expected she would move back in with me but all the years of trying to foster a sense of independence continued to pay off. She had spent several summers in Lake Placid in upstate New York attending a skating camp. She now decided against all the advice of her teachers and school counselors to leave Cambridge and live full-time in Lake Placid.

That was a big step in her life. I listened to the teachers and thought their reasoning was valid: she would be amongst friends and classmates in Cambridge, and the school would help her with employment. But I also listened to Allegra. Up until this point, every big decision in her life had been made by others. This was now her time, and I agreed to let her pursue her skating dreams. She lived with her coach and competed in the Adult Nationals (where again, most had no idea she had learning disabilities). She discovered a newfound sense of freedom in her decision. Oftentimes her coach had to travel and she would remain behind in a big old house all by herself. I fretted, of course. How would she manage? Who would cook? Who would do her laundry? The answer to all these questions was Allegra herself.

Eventually, she did leave Lake Placid and decided to move back to Cambridge. A few years later she met a young man named Josh

Thomas. Eventually she became Mrs. Allegra Ford Thomas, and they live a happy, peaceful life in the Boston area.

I could not be happier or more proud of her achievements. Allegra's life as an independent adult did not come easily for her or for me, but every tear, every bit of self-doubt, and every moment of the countless hours spent on teaching her to advocate for herself has paid off in the end.

I still have twitches of embarrassment when she says something that makes no sense, but as always, it is *me* that has the embarrassment. Allegra isn't embarrassed. Her husband isn't embarrassed. No one else is embarrassed. A sense of stigma comes my way and it is always, *always* a most unwelcome guest – and so I tell myself to knock it off and on we go.

And on we go now, to other mothers, to young adults with LD, and to the professionals, who can help shine a light upon stigma – and though none of us may fully eradicate it from society, we at least have a good chance of lessening its effects on our children and ourselves.

Mothers and Their Children

Navigating Through the Mine-fields of Stigma

When I thought of a metaphor for stigma, I tried to think of what it was like for a parent, the constant worry, the unexpected shocks, the expectations of something coming at you from out of the blue; and I came up with the image of a minefield. Truly, I think this image covers so many things with LD. Parents are continually on the lookout for unforeseen difficulties. Sometimes these difficulties creep up on us. Other times they come with alarming suddenness. In either case, life can be turned upside down in no time at all, especially in the early days of a child's diagnosis.

Let's say you're picking up your child from school. It's the same scene that replays day after day, with very little change. Suddenly you hear a schoolyard taunt floating on the wind – "Retard!" Your child may not respond, and that brings its own pain when you realize this is a name he or she has heard before and is used to it. But for the mother, oh my goodness. Words can come like arrows, and sink in as deep as an arrow too.

One mother told me, "When it comes to stigma, the child is often the target but might not realize it. The parents *do* realize it, and they get stigmatized too. We're bad, negligent parents because we try to show some semblance of normalcy in public. When something goes awry, we get the looks of disapproval and realize there are some 'friends' we'll never hear from again. Think about the things people write on Facebook about people bringing children to restaurants. You see it all the time, complaints about the disruption and the noise. Now factor in special needs and, but for the rarest of humans, we see the disapproval times twenty – and that happens even when the kids don't misbehave!"

Going to a restaurant. A walk in the park. A first day of school. For children with special needs and their parents, such simple, everyday occurrences hold within them the possibility of stigma appearing without prior notice.

THE GATEWAY SCHOOL

When I decided to speak to mothers who deal with the issues of stigma and social skills on a regular basis, I thought a good place to start would be with some mothers whose children attend Allegra's old school, The Gateway School in New York City. It has changed so much over the years since my daughter went there. The school is no longer made of makeshift classrooms at the edges of an old gymnasium as I described in my own story. It is now housed in a gorgeous building and looks like very much like a school any child could go to, regardless of whether or not that child had special needs.

I met with three mothers in an unused classroom one winter's day. They sat on one side of a long table while I sat on the other. They were Valerie, who has a ten year old daughter named Olivia, born with severe LD.

Beside her sat Rosemary, also with a daughter with LD named Samantha (with the nickname "Sam"). Sam is in 7th grade at Gateway. Her diagnoses include ADHD, dysgraphia, LD-NOS and Anxiety-Disorder-NOS (NOS, Not Otherwise Specified, means she doesn't specifically fit the classic definitions of these conditions. Dysgraphia is a learning disability that affects writing.)

Last was Suzanne, whose thirteen-year-old son Gregory suffers from severe ADHD.

I began the discussion of stigma by asking if anyone had any initial thoughts about society's reaction to individuals with LD or the stigma a child with LD feels about their own disability.

Valerie said, "I think I feel the stigma more than my daughter Olivia does, which makes me hover even more than I normally would. I do this to prevent her from figuring out that she is getting 'dissed' socially. Ever since she was a baby, I have spent a lot of time trying to protect her from the cruelty of others, and when it comes, she is blessedly unaware. Now that she is getting older I think she is getting more sensitized to it. People judge, and people are mean, and I think some people who might otherwise be nice to her just don't know what to do."

"They don't know how to respond to her or what to say?" I asked.

"Right. Cruelty might be too strong a word for that type of person. It's more that people pull back a little bit. If we're on a playground, you can see that people leave her alone."

"Children?"

"Both children and adults," Valerie said. "They might be afraid she will fall down, or whatever her issues are of the day. They don't understand what's going on. They don't know how to relate to her. She is very slow to speak. Children wonder what that means: in their minds, she is too big to not be able to speak clearly. My daughter is very friendly and outgoing, so she never shrinks back from anything that anyone might say to her. She's still like that, even though she still has the speech problems. But as we go down this road, I feel I'm not going to be front and center and the first line of defense for her forever....and that kills me."

"It kills you because you think the stigma will never go away?"

"Yes," Valerie said. "And it's not that I think the stigma will never go away – I *know* it won't. Honestly, I think people are rotten. I really do. Kids are rotten to each other. I'm in a parenting moment right now which is very difficult. I started a Brownies group and a Girl Scout troop. I did it to help create a social network for my daughter with disabilities. I did not do it for all the other rotten girls who have me climbing up trees, and organizing camping trips, and this, that, and the other thing. I did it to provide a weekly gathering for Olivia. She has loved it and it's been great, but I am four years into it. We have our little meetings and everyone goes their own way, and there are sleepovers being arranged and birthday parties; and I can't take it anymore. She is not included in *any* of them. She just isn't. So the stigma is right there in plain sight. I don't think she expects to be included, but *I* expect her to be included."

"Does your daughter ever ask the others to come over and spend the night only for the girls to say no?"

"No, but only because I will direct her to the one nice girl who might say yes. But now I feel like I really can't tell her to ask the nice one all the time, because that girl is not going to want to come. If she says yes, it's only because she's nice, not because she really wants to."

"What about the girls in her class here at school?" I asked.

"Last year I was all over it because it was our first year here. I think it's a very inclusive community because we're all in the same boat, but the unexpected thing is this: everyone is on their own little journey. So, for example, Olivia doesn't like the dark, and she's not good at sleepovers, and she doesn't like it when people have cats *and* dogs – it's a bunch of things. Everyone in the school has their own separate issues like that. So this is what happens: you find a compatible group of kids who like each other and they have a ball, but they can't do the same things all the time. Last year I did an awful lot to mix and mingle, but I realized everyone has their own bag of issues, so we don't mesh all that easily. Everyone is going five days a week, with appointments and tutors and this and that."

"I assume summer is also a problem, when she doesn't have the classmates around."

"Yes," Valerie said, "so last summer she started going to camp."

"A summer camp for children with LD?"

"Yes. I bit the bullet and enrolled her."

"That's the best thing you could do," I said. "I did it too. It was incredibly hard to see Allegra go off to camp but it was a huge step toward her independence."

"I think I aimed low to get Olivia to the next step, which might be a higher functioning place. I don't think this camp is perfect, but it is incredibly supportive. Even so, I would like to see her in a more up-and-at-'em camp. The kids in this camp need an awful lot of hand-holding."

I asked the group if any family member or neighborhood friend ever said anything negative about their child.

Rosemary said, "I feel stigma a lot because my daughter Samantha is now in 7th grade, and I find that other family members or friends have started to make assumptions. For instance, they'll say, 'Oh, if she's in 7th grade, she must be doing this and this.' And she's not. She doesn't have a cell phone yet because she doesn't go anywhere by herself and she doesn't like to be home alone at all. Everyone makes the assumption that I can just leave her home sometimes. I remember a family friend saying, "oh, I know of a sleep-away camp," but no. She can't do that."

"Did this family friend know there was an issue with your daughter?" I asked.

"No. In fairness, this is a friend who was new to the family – but there are definitely people who know the family well who make assumptions. They'll say things like, "In only a few years Sam will be in college," and I think, "No, I don't think we know that at all.""

"So is it fair to say you feel the sense of stigma more than your daughter does?"

"I do," Rosemary said, "although I think she gets a little thrown when someone asks her about things she doesn't do. She'll say to me, 'I don't do that…is that OK?' And I say, 'Of course! Everyone does things differently.' I really try to shrug it off and to get her to shrug it off too. For myself, there are aspects of her disabilities that have caused difficulties in my life. She has coordination issues and attention issues, so I have to help her shower a couple times a week and…" Here Rosemary broke down a bit and began to cry. "Sorry."

"It's ok," I said. "It still happens to me and my child is forty!"

Rosemary continued through her tears, "But you know, you just sort of ask yourself, 'She is in 7th grade, should I still be doing this?' And then my husband says, 'If she had physical disabilities, you wouldn't hesitate. You would say 'Of course I would help her in the shower. Of course I would tie her shoes on the street.' When I think of myself, I think I'm accepting of my daughter's disability. I'm comfortable with it and I'm very active at the school and in getting people to talk about it openly, but there are some parents who don't even want to talk about it here at the school. Some refuse to call it a disability. They prefer to call it a learning difference – and it's *not*. It's so much more than a difference. But there comes a point where…again, if it was physical, I wouldn't have a problem at all."

Suzanne said, "My son Gregory has very severe ADHD, which ends up being his disability. It is so severe that it inhibits everything he does. If we're driving and he suddenly blurts out 'I gotta have some water, I gotta have some water' or whatever, and I get upset, my husband says, 'Suzanne, if he had diabetes, you'd stop and take his blood sugar.' And I'm like, 'Yeah, but I have two other kids in the car.' How much of your life can be controlled by one child when you have two others? But the reality is this: I have a child who has been completely stigmatized, and has been all of his life."

"Where was he before he came to Gateway?"

"He was at a very good mainstream school until this year. Academically he's always been fine. Right now we're struggling because he's doing his schoolwork as he's walking down the hall. We have no issues academically. He's very bright. That has not been a problem in school. But he's unable to contain himself. In school, he's on medication. The teachers in his other school loved him until he went to 4th grade. At that point they changed in their perceptions of him. They didn't understand him. They seemed to think he should have been able to control himself by that age."

"Have you ever had a family member say there is nothing wrong with him?"

"Yes. There have been grandparents who said that. My father would say, 'Why didn't you just slap him on the bottom when he was younger?' and 'Why don't you spank him?' So, yeah, sure, they said that sort of thing. I also have two other children who are really accepting of him. But he's the big brother and…"

"You think its harder that he's the eldest?"

"No," Suzanne said. "In fact, I think sometimes it's harder to be the youngest. The eldest has the benefit of having two younger people who look up to him. I know a family who has twins and a younger child who has all the problems. It's very difficult because the two older girls forget the younger sister. They're much older now. The twins are twenty-four and the younger one is twenty-one. And it's like they forget about her. They forget to include her. In my family, my other two children are understanding. Every once in a while my youngest child will say something about Gregory, but never anything like 'you're weird.' If I take Gregory off his medication, the younger one will joke around and say things like, 'Did you take your medication yet?' But he never says anything that will really hit hard."

Rosemary said, "My kids will tell Samantha that she's acting weird, but they'll never say she *is* weird. They'll call her out on her behavior, and thank God she has that because sometimes you need a sibling to just give it to you."

"I agree with that," I said. "It's good to have that balance and sometimes a sibling can do things in a blunt necessary way that no one else can."

"I also have a few issues with family members regarding stigma issues," Rosemary said. "My father-in-law will say things, for instance. I always try to make sure that I explain things to them ahead of time so they understand what's going on if she has a fit at a holiday dinner or we have to leave something early. Even so, he'll say things like, 'If she would come live with me, everything would be fine.' And I'm like, 'Really? You think so?' After hearing it about twelve times, you finally realize they don't understand and maybe can't understand."

"Have they ever come to see the school?"

"They will come this year for Grandparents Day. This will be the first time. But even without that, my father-in-law is slowly beginning to understand."

I asked Valerie if she had any issues with stigma when it came to other family members.

"Yes. The form of stigma from my extended family that rubs me the wrong way is when they say things like, 'She's just a baby.' She's *not* just a baby. She is almost eleven and she is infantilized by everyone. And she just revels in the idea that she's not able to do everything that everyone else can. I can't stand it because I think the message she gets is that she's not capable in any way. They say it in a caring and concerned kind of way, but you know what? You have to buck this kid up. She has to stand up and she's got to stay with the pack. If we're at a family gathering I might say to my daughter, 'Go back and get your bag and bring it here.' And if they're all going swimming and she forgot her towel, she's got to go back and get it. I sometimes think it makes me look like I'm being hard on her."

"That's an interesting comment," Suzanne said. "It seems no matter happens, the mother is *always* the problem."

"I don't get it!" Valerie said, frustrated.

"I make a point to say that," Suzanne continued, "because no matter what happens, it's always my fault. No matter what."

"And yet what would they do without you?" I asked.

"Even with the kids who don't have the LD," Suzanne said, "you always feel like you're doing the wrong thing. No matter what, you never feel you're giving them enough time. But it's so classic...because even the one you are hovering over feels that way."

I asked the mothers if they ever felt a sense of stigma because their child is enrolled in a special school.

"Gregory had a terrible time changing schools," Suzanne said, "especially when people would ask him where he was going. They would do the same with me. People ask which school he's going to, and rather than explain, I would say, 'it's a new school.'

"That was definitely my experience when Allegra went here," I said. "It was a huge challenge for me, dealing with those questions. But nowadays there are so many children in these schools I can't believe there is still a stigma."

"Oh yes, there is totally a stigma," Valerie said. She turned to the others and asked, "Do you ever get the sad face when you tell them your child goes to a special school or is in special education, like 'Oh, I'm sorry to hear that.'? That drives me crazy. But I sometimes get a positive reaction from people who say they know someone else whose child goes to Gateway."

Rosemary said, "I get the parents whose kids are in private or public schools who take me aside and whisper, 'We're looking at other schools, can you meet me for coffee?' What this means is they need to send their child to a school like Gateway. They say it like it's a secret they don't want anyone to hear."

"I got that yesterday!" Valerie said.

"They don't want anyone to know," Rosemary continued. "Or they've had the big meeting at school where they were just told their child has LD. I always say to these parents, 'Don't make this about your kid. Make it about the school. Ask yourself if that school is good enough to deal with your child. If not, find a better place.'"

"Which matters more in this school?" I asked. "Socialization or academics?"

Rosemary said, "Socialization. We just went to my daughter's psychiatrist. We brought in some of her homework and we were looking at it....her handwriting is terrible, the sentences are so simple, and we can all see that she has not progressed that much academically. She's done Occupational Therapy for five or six years, but she still doesn't cross the midline and her spelling is atrocious. I can grill her and grill her and make her stress out, but she simply can't retain it, so right now I'm letting the school do their thing with socialization."

Valerie said, "Olivia transferred here last year from a mainstream school and the word that I got from everyone at Gateway was that the first year was her 'recovery year'. By that they meant they were going back two steps to a point before she had problems at the other school. They were bucking her up. They were making her feel stronger as a math student and a reading student, but I couldn't help feeling that going backward in 7th grade couldn't be good, because

Gateway only has students through 8th grade and, after that, we'll have to move on to a different school. I think a year is a long time to 'recover', and honestly, I didn't think she was so battle-weary from her previous experience, but there was no talking anyone out of the plan at Gateway. I think she lost a full year academically last year and that's what keeps me up at night. She's socialized in every way. I think she's blossomed in that area and, in the book of life, that is a very important thing. But she still needs to know her times tables."

Rosemary said, "I really struggle with the question, 'How much can my child really learn?' My daughter lacks maturity. She's in 7th grade and playing with Barbie dolls, and the very little homework she is given is enough. She can't really handle anything else. We can't do play-dates, though we're working on it."

Suzanne said, "I know my son Gregory can learn because, in the past, he never had a problem with the academic side of things. But socially it's difficult. He doesn't have a friend. He prefers to do schoolwork at lunch over having lunch with others. He doesn't know how to make a phone call. He's not unpleasant. He's a very nice kid, but he doesn't know how to respond when someone is calling him. So yes, he's totally losing his academics here. He never sees homework. Never."

"And he doesn't want to eat lunch with the others because he doesn't know how to socialize?"

"Yes. That's why he always wants the working lunch. He doesn't know how to socialize, so they're trying to find him a 'partner-friend' to have lunch with him. But he still manages to get into the working lunch by saying he has homework, even though he doesn't have homework at all. He's making that up as an excuse. So it's very awkward."

Rosemary said, "There is also a problem when the parents of a child with special needs are super-high functioning and extremely organized. They have difficulties with all of this. I don't think I ever was that in my life, so I'm more accepting."

"You think the parents here are high functioning?"

"Some are, yes."

"I'm not," Suzanne said. "I went to Yale. I was a top student in public high school but at Yale I struggled so much. I vowed I was not going to do that to my kids. It was the wrong place for me. It was too hard for me. Even so, I am disturbed by the fact that my son went from having homework in his old school to having none now. I don't want them to think I'm a nut, but he's got to have something to do at night."

"Have you told them?"

"Oh yes, I write to them every week, but it doesn't change."

There is always some tension between academic and social development when it comes to children with LD. We, as parents, try to put an emphasis on both, but there are times when our concerns about one outweigh the other (I will discuss this in the next chapter with the head of the Gateway School, Dr. Robert Cunningham.) In this conversation with the mothers, I wanted to get their views on this balance between academics and socialization. "Is it fair to say you believe the biggest challenge in your child's life is friendships?" I asked.

"It depends," Rosemary said. "When Samantha is in the school environment here at Gateway, she does fantastically well. She has ADHD and talks a lot, and sometimes she'll just go on and on and on. Because of coordination, she won't play sports, but she will talk excessively and that's okay here at Gateway."

"I can understand that friendships are a little easier when most of their classmates have similar issues," I said, "but what happens outside the school?"

"That's when it gets hard," Rosemary said. "You know, you're in conversation with someone and Samantha starts going off on another subject; and you kind of get 'the look'. If it's someone around her age, you get the look that they know something isn't quite right. That is difficult."

"Valerie said she sent her daughter to summer camp," I said to Rosemary. "Have you ever sent Samantha to camp?"

"She's been attending a mainstream camp, and has been doing that for a while."

"And it's worked out for her?"

"Well…no," Rosemary admitted. "It's a day camp. Every year I have to talk to the counselors. Socially, Samantha hangs out with the counselors more than the other girls. They'll say things like, 'I feel very sorry for her because she doesn't seem to have many friends, but when we ask the kids if they want to come back the next year, she's always the first one to raise her hand.' She loves it. And for me, I view it as a chance to be with a larger group of girls her own age. There aren't that many in her grade here at Gateway. She does have one friend at camp who goes to another LD school and is working on her own issues.

37

They do clash sometimes. For instance, Sam gets all cozy and weepy, but this girl gets a little mean and hard. Even so, there are usually no problems with her. And in terms of social development, one of the things I asked the counselors was if girls are shaving their legs in 7th grade. She's my oldest so I really didn't know. The counselor said they are, and recommended that Samantha do the same. So I said to Sam, 'You know, some girls are shaving their legs so maybe you ought to think about it before camp. I'm fine with whatever you want.' She wasn't going for it at all and I said that's totally fine. So she went off to camp, came home, and said: 'Mom, we've got to shave my legs.' That's a good example of socialization. By surrounding her with those other children, she learned."

I said, "My daughter will insist that she had lots of friends when she was younger, when she really didn't."

"Samantha is like that. Everyone is Samantha's friend."

"There really does seem to be a lack of awareness that there's a problem," I said. "Allegra never had a group of girls to hang out with, or go to the movies with. She never had that until she went to high school, but to this day she will insist she had lots of friends. I'm happy about that. It always seemed worse for me than it did for her. Do you ever feel that?"

"Absolutely!" Valerie said.

Rosemary agreed. "Yes, because we pick up on every little social thing. We see the roll of the eyes. We see the back turned."

I noticed Suzanne shaking her head. "You don't agree?" I asked.

"No," she said. "I think its worse for my son because he knows things in his other school were not so good. Now that he's here, he knows things are better. But I think he's fully aware of how bad things were. He was terribly bullied last year and I think he realizes it was because he had problems due to his disability. He's good looking, he's tall, he's a good athlete, he's not the picture of a kid who gets bullied. But he was really badly bullied. He never knew how to join a group. He didn't know how to fit in. Since pre-school he's been like that. The pre-school teacher said, 'Gregory doesn't quite know what to do. The others are playing cops and robbers and he didn't know how to fit in.' If someone said he was to be a robber, he would say he wanted to be a cop. He didn't know how to say, 'OK'. He'd say, 'OK, but I want to do this,' and the others wouldn't want to do what he wanted, and that would be the end of it. He didn't know how to join."

As our conversation ended, we all agreed there were no easy answers to the problems caused by stigma. Are there ways to avoid it? Or ways to lessen the pain?

The mothers at Gateway had few concrete answers. I didn't either.

But these are the questions I continue to ask throughout this book and the ones I eventually hope to answer.

"YOUR FAMILY IS ONLY AS HAPPY AS YOUR UNHAPPIEST CHILD"

A Conversation on Social Skills and Stigma with Dr. Robert Cunningham

Moving on from the conversation with the Gateway mothers, we know that every parent wants their child to have friends and a fun, fulfilling time in and out of school. Having said that, have some parents lost sight of the importance of their child having friends?

I posed this question to Robert Cunningham, Ed.M., in a conversation about stigma, social skills and how parents can best care for their child who may be experiencing these challenges. Dr. Cunningham serves as advisor-in-residence on learning disabilities and attention issues for Understood, an organization affiliated with the National Center for Learning Disabilities. He is also head of school at the Robert Louis Stevenson School (though our conversation took place when he was head of the Gateway School).

I visited him at in his office on the same day I spoke with the mothers in the previous chapter. When I pulled up to the front of the school, a group of young teenaged girls walked past, laughing and joking about something. "It was a perfectly ordinary scene," I told Dr. Cunningham when I joined him in his office. "It was exactly the sort of thing you would expect in front of a school, and yet my *first thought* was, 'Oh, Allegra never had that.' Even after all these years, it still haunts me. She never got called to go out and have a soda with someone, or go to a movie with a group of friends. It never happened. And that's sad. I don't honestly know whether or not Allegra knew it was sad, but it certainly was sad for me."

"It *is* sad," he said. "It's sad for everyone. Some children with special needs may not be affected by a lack of friends, but most will. Social development is really tough and I think it's getting more difficult all the time. Some of the changes going on in education and society could be doing more harm than good for children with LD – mostly because they are changes in thinking on the part of the parent. The culture of education has shifted so far to a quantitative bent. Everything that parents are taught to value or that parents are encouraged to value has to do with immediate impact. They are encouraged to value results they can see, such as measurable grades and test scores. The problem is that social development doesn't respond well to that approach. You can lay out a curriculum map for science. You can lay out one for reading skills. It's really hard to do that for social development, so the way parents look at academic learning is not meshing well with the way kids develop social competence."

"Was it not like that in the past?"

"No, it wasn't, because a lot of things were assessed qualitatively rather than quantitatively, and more through description. Now everything is brought down to a symbol or a letter or a number, and you really can't do that with social development. Parents today are having a harder time grasping how these things are addressed, and *why* they're addressed. I can spend fifteen minutes with you and give you a really good understanding of how your child is reading, but I can't even come close to giving you a good understanding of how your child is developing socially."

"Do parents expect you to be able to do that?" I asked.

"They either expect you to be able to do that, or it doesn't even enter into their minds when they're talking to the teachers. The whole notion that social development is something that needs to be addressed thoroughly and continually at a school is not in the mix anymore."

Needless to say, I found this disturbing. I wondered aloud if it was because parents don't think of social competence as a legitimate issue to be addressed in the school, or if they separate it so much from the academics that they don't think of it as a school issue.

"We have a social development program here that flows through everything we do at the school, but even so, when we talk to families and attempt to talk thoroughly about social development, we are often met with a good deal of frustration. They'll say, 'Well, OK, that's nice, but how is he doing in reading?' Or they might say, 'Every year I hear that my child is progressing socially and that everyone is so happy with it, but I'm still concerned that he can't read a periodic table.' So you see, there is a definite trend toward weighting academic achievement over the social domain of learning."

"And that's what gets you through life," I said. "Social skills, not reading a periodic table."

"Absolutely! And when we survey our graduates, social skills are always at the top of their list. When you ask them what has allowed them to be successful, they'll say, 'It's because I learned how to manage friendships and how to advocate for myself.' We might then ask about something like science, and they'll say, 'Well, anyone can learn science as long as you have a good teacher and a good book, but if I didn't know how to work cooperatively with my classmates, and if I didn't know how to tell the teacher that I needed something repeated in a different way, I wouldn't have been successful.'"

"And when you tell this to parents, do they get it?"

"Most do," Dr. Cunningham said with some hesitation. "They get it, but it's still not what they're jumping to first."

"Maybe they're worried about the competition their child will face once they're out in the world. Even if that is the case, I would think social development would continue to be one of their top concerns."

"On one level it is," Dr. Cunningham said. "They'll say, 'Gosh, the most important thing to me is that my kid be happy and have friends.' We'll talk a little bit about that, and about social skills and social development, but it won't be long before they'll say, 'Well, that's nice, but are they going to be prepared for a high school math class?' I understand that concern – I really do, but the pendulum has definitely swung very far in that direction."

I would never discount the importance of academics, but at the same time, I do wonder at their value when *only* academics are involved. Imagine a person who is completely illiterate but has wonderful social skills. This was much more common in the past than today, but even then, many, if not most of them, sailed through life. They couldn't read or weren't good with math, but they were still successful because they were socially successful.

Social skills are of primary importance. Parents *know* this. You know it – I know it – everyone knows it. I've said it before, but it bears repeating over and over: stigma very often comes about due to a lack of social skills. Even so, some parents seem to have drifted away from this position, as if somehow a focus on social skills would take time away from the all-important test scores.

Dr. Cunningham said, "It takes courage these days for a parent to say, 'I understand my child needs these kinds of social development priorities in order to be successful. I also understand the academics are going to come, because I'm confident that if my child has these social skills, no matter what he's expected to do in a learning environment, he'll figure out a way through. He'll master that. If he's not reading by the time he's in sixth grade, he'll read when he's in seventh or eighth grade, but right now, I know that social development needs to be the priority.' That's really tough for a parent to say. It takes a huge amount of courage. But I really want to stress this: without the social development, the academic skill development and the content knowledge are not meaningful. Without a foundation of social development and social skills, no matter how much you know and no matter what you can do, you're not going to be happy and successful. It's not going to happen unless you have learned how to relate to others. Gateway has a strong focus on social development, though of course we do focus on academics as well."

I told him of something told to me by Rick Lavoie, former headmaster of the Riverview School on Cape Cod. We had been discussing how challenges with social skills can be so difficult for a child and Rick told me it can be just as difficult for the parent. "No parent has ever come into my office crying about low math scores," he said. "It is the lack of friends that breaks a parent's heart."

"That's how it *was*," Dr. Cunningham said, "but now they come in crying over low math scores. For many parents, grades are more important than the social issues."

For the mother or father reading this now, I ask you these questions: do you see yourself in any of this? Do you tend to overlook or downplay the social development side in favor of grades and test scores? The crying in the office may have changed, but the situation has not. The math scores may be low, but the most pressing worry for any child is the lack of friends.

I told Dr. Cunningham I found his words about this a little distressing. "Especially when the problems with social skills are something that parents see every day," I said. "It would be extremely obvious that their child can't play with anyone, or has no friends."

"But you know what? If I could post great test scores from a child who has social disabilities, the parents would be very pleased."

"So it's a little like thinking art and music classes are nice, but let's get rid of them because what we really need is an algebra class."

"Correct," Dr. Cunningham said. "And if you dismiss the quality of learning that takes place through the arts, it's not hard to dismiss the importance of social development. It's going to take really courageous families and really courageous schools to continue to address social development."

"But what about the everyday effects of social problems?" I asked. "There are times when a child who has social development problems will say something inappropriate, or act in inappropriate ways. To be blunt about it, this can be embarrassing for the parents."

"They *are* embarrassed," Dr. Cunningham said. "But there are other forms of embarrassment to take into consideration. One of them is the embarrassment some parents feel when saying their child goes to a special school, or is in special education. If a mother can say, 'My child goes to a school for children with special needs," and she suffers through the painful silence while the other person processes what she just said, and she can then follow that up with, 'But he got a high score on his math test in third grade,' – then everyone around her will say, 'oh, he's really good at math!' Suddenly the conversation has shifted away from the topic of special education to what your child does well and what you can be proud of."

"So unless the child is embarrassing the family by something they're doing at that particular moment, the social skills problems are quickly out of mind."

Dr. Cunningham agreed. "We have families who rationally know that social development is of primary importance, but emotionally they have a hard time with it. But in the end, if the child is unhappy, the family is unhappy. One of my trustees always says, your family is only as happy as your unhappiest child. It's true, and everybody knows it's true, but when they talk to the school about what's important, that's not what they talk about."

"The interesting thing is that I do hear a lot of parents talk about it," I said, "but maybe that's because it's in a different environment. When I speak to parent groups, they don't usually talk about their child's academics but more about family issues."

"Those issues resonate with people," Dr. Cunningham said. "They *know* those issues. They experience them every day, but when they go to their parent/teacher conference, that's not what they talk about. It's difficult for some people to grasp that you have a certain number of hours in a school day, which means that a school has to prioritize how they're going to use those hours for the betterment of the child. I think it is less and less acceptable for a school to say 'we're going to spend 80% of our time on social development because we believe it's critical for future happiness.' I don't think a lot of families would tolerate that type of explanation. They want you to address it, but the idea that you would think to stress social development ahead of academic development is something that is so anathema to the way they've been inculturated to think about education that it's just too big a barrier for them to get past."

"I assume that attitude can be reflected in school budgets too," I said. "When a school district is having trouble financially, often the first things to go are the art and music classes and maybe even sports, and unfortunately those are sometimes the lifelines for children with LD."

"They are, yes. The arts and technology."

"And this doesn't help with social issues because it takes away an avenue that would really help them."

"Here at Gateway, we have a whole strand of our program that focuses on Interest Identification and Talent Development, because you know that the child who has a passion or an interest in a particular thing is more successful socially. Why? Because they can relate to someone else on a real level, about something of shared interest."

"I always encourage parents to do that," I said. "I urge them to help find the child's interest, no matter what it is. That passion or interest can really lead to a more fulfilling social life. That's what skating was for Allegra."

"Exactly. Skating for Allegra is a perfect example. In those sorts of environments, nobody cares if someone has LD or not. It doesn't matter. When our kids here are competing against other teams in the Leggo Robotics competition in the city, nobody cares if they're from a special ed school. What they care about is that the robot can do some cool thing that they should have thought of."

"It's important not to minimize those achievements and activities."

"When you do minimize them, the whole social domain falls apart for the kid," Dr. Cunningham said. "On the other hand, if there is adequate focus on the social domain, then by the time a child gets to high school, they can identify much more by what they're good at than what they have trouble with. Having said all that, it never happens for a lot of kids."

This was a disheartening, yet realistic, view of the lack of emphasis on social development, even in schools for children with special needs. Social skills are being put on a back burner – sometimes by the school, sometimes by the parent. For parents to become an effective advocate for their child they must focus on their child's needs. For some, this may mean taking action within the school. They may have to join or lead a fight to keep the arts and sports program from being cut, and this may mean joining forces with other parents.

Why does this matter so much?

For many children with LD, the arts, sports and technology become their key to unlock the possibilities for future happiness. They can also help alleviate the effects of stigma.

I asked Dr. Cunningham for his views on this. "First of all, I think stigma affects both the parent and the child," he began. "In terms of the child, there seems to be a point in every student's life where stigma becomes an issue. Some kids get through age eight or nine without ever having dealt with the fact that they are different from other kids. They don't encounter it until middle school, or even later. Other kids deal with it right away when they get to a school like Gateway. We'll have a six year old ask 'Is this a special school?' Or 'Is this school different from other schools?' or they'll ask why they have to be in a school like this. We have classes and courses that are specifically designed to address that with the kids. It's called Myself as a Learner. They learn about themselves as learners, and other people as learners. It gives them a good full picture, so when they get to high school they're well aware of their challenges and are able to discuss and advocate for themselves."

"And the parents?"

"Believe it or not, stigma is often much more difficult for the parents, especially when they have a child in special education or in a school for children with LD."

"One of the ongoing problems is a lack of belief that there is even such a thing as learning disabilities," I said. "I recently brought up the subject of LD with a doctor, a general practitioner. He hesitated a bit and said he didn't really believe there is such a thing. Remember, this was a doctor. He said he thought LD and autism were due to eating too much junk food, too much Coke and potato chips. I was shocked – he was completely ignorant about the issue, and he was a doctor."

"It happens all the time," said Dr. Cunningham. "Teachers of children with LD sometimes get offended because the first thing people will say to them is, 'Oh, you must have a lot of patience.' The teachers say, 'I do, but I also happen to have advanced degrees and an awful lot of knowledge.' So there is definitely a stigma attached. We also face it in placement process here at the school. We hear about other mainstream schools that will directly say to a child, 'So you have a learning disability, do you think you could fit in with the other kids here?' Essentially, they are saying in a not very subtle way, "Do you really think you can make it here in this school?" It's worse around social difficulties because they try to figure out clever ways to talk to the child about what they think about friendship and what they think about social development things…basically, in their mind, they're trying to figure out if the kid is weird."

"Is the stigma the same, worse, or better for LD as opposed to Special Education?" I asked. "In other words, if someone hears a child has LD, do they think of that as something apart from Special Ed?"

"The only issue I believe is viewed with little to no stigma is the one where parent advocacy has been strongest, and that is dyslexia. People have come to accept the term dyslexia as 'nothing really wrong'."

"Anybody will say they have dyslexia without hesitation." I said. "Attention Deficit Disorder too. I feel the term *Special Ed* is a problem. I've always felt that. I say it in all my books, and often when I speak. The word *special* has lost its meaning. In fact, for many people, when it comes to education, the word special means quite the opposite. In their mind it indicates that particular person is singled out in a dismissive, non-special way."

"Most of our kids will say in their Myself as a Learner courses that if people ask if they have dyslexia, they'll just say Yes. They won't say that about other learning disabilities. Some will say it even if they're nowhere near having dyslexia. They vastly prefer to say dyslexia rather than LD or special needs."

"So again we have the issue with the word *special.*"

"You get all kinds of strange comments about Special Ed, and the kids have to deal with that and the parents have to deal with that — it's a lot for them. Sometimes we get parents who don't even want to tell the school that their child has special needs. They will withhold information about their child's disabilities. In that case, there is also the issue of the explanation itself. Parents get weighed down by always having to explain their child. The children get weighed down by it too. 'What grade are you in?' another child will ask. 'I don't know, my school's an ungraded school.' 'What do you mean it's an ungraded school? Why is it an ungraded school?' And they will have to explain over and over. Or the question might be, "How many kids are in your class?" and they'll have to explain why they only have eight. Or they'll ask, "What are you studying?""

"When you have the graduates come back to talk to current students, do they say that they still have a disability?" I asked.

"They do, yes."

"Allegra often says she *used to* have LD but doesn't anymore."

Dr. Cunningham said, "One of the guys who had ADD said he's much more able to regulate it now and that it doesn't affect him like it used to…though it's still not easy for him."

"We sometimes find young adults with LD who don't want to associate with others with similar disabilities, especially those who may look more disabled than most."

"We have that a lot with parents too. They want to see the class before they make the decision to send their child there — but it's not really the class they want to see. They want to see the other kids in the class to make sure they're not 'funny looking'. There are some kids here who have obvious syndrome types of things, but most do not."

"Is it the parent who really wants to see the other students? Or is it the child who wants to see his or her classmates?"

"It's the parent."

"Have you ever had a parent say this wasn't the right place for them?"

"Yes, at middle school level we have had that. I can think of two times it happened, but both times, we had the child come back to spend a full day here and they ended up enrolling."

I brought up the issue of bullying and what I thought to be my rather unorthodox take on it. "I've been asked a couple of times if Allegra had been bullied in school," I told him. "My answer is this: I wish she had been. It sounds crazy, I know, but at least someone would have paid attention to her."

"I understand what you mean," he said. "It's the same when a child at Gateway presents a discipline problem for the first time. The parents don't see it as a problem but as a cause for celebration. The child was aware enough to know his action would be unacceptable and he did it anyway, just to see what would happen. Now he feels bad about it. That kind of misbehavior can actually be a milestone in child development."

"Yes, and my statement about the bullying – how sad it is to think that for someone who is not paid attention to at all, bullying could be seen as an improvement."

"That goes into behavioral psychology," Dr. Cunningham said. "Any attention is good attention. That's why a lot of kids seek negative attention because they're not getting the other kind, no matter what they do."

"And think about that, how sad that is," I said again, wrapping up our conversation. "That a child can be so ignored that they actively search out stigma, simply to be noticed."

"HE'S PERFECT. BUT HE'S DIFFERENT"

The Craig School

We will now hear from a couple of mothers who have found ways to help their children handle the stigma that comes their way. I met them during a discussion at the Craig School, a school in Mountain Lakes, New Jersey that specializes in working with students with learning disabilities in grades two through twelve. We had a broad-ranging conversation, but I would like to focus now upon their methods and attitudes that led to their children's empowerment and acceptance – this is not to say the mothers at the previous school, Gateway, did not, or could not, use these methods, only that I am putting an emphasis on the solutions in this conversation rather than the problems. Mostly, it's an attitude, a way of looking at their child that deflects stigma away through focusing on the positive.

Sally

I have the gift of having a cousin who is my age and has dyslexia. They didn't diagnose anything until he was seventeen. I say it was a gift because when my son Peter wouldn't color inside the lines in preschool, I thought that was a little strange. When he got to kindergarten and he couldn't identify the letters, I thought that was very bizarre. I thought this because he was my first child and, like

51

many new parents, we vowed we would never watch TV around him and we would only read books. We actually did that until he was two, but then he got pneumonia and he was in the hospital and, honestly, I could not read another book. All I wanted was a bottle of wine and a box of chocolate and I was totally ready to let him watch Nickelodeon. It turned out he didn't really like TV and he didn't like video games, so we continued to read to him a lot. This is why I could not understand why he did not know his letters. We read to him all the time, every night, and we had every wall in his bedroom decorated with letters from the alphabet. And what did the kindergarten teach say to me over and over again? "You need to read to him more often."

We then got to first grade and he went from being an average student to being at the bottom of the class, and the teacher sat there and told me my seven year old wasn't trying. An evaluator tested him and told us that our son could not be educated and that he would never be able to read or write like a normal human. That's what they said to me. She tried to tell me there was a physical reason for it. Peter has food allergies, so he can go into shock if he ate many things that we would normally eat. The evaluator asked if it was possible that he had an allergic episode without me knowing. I said, "Well, no, because he would have died." She continued on with her theory. She said, "It may be possible that he had one that you didn't know about because we think he think he is probably brain damaged."

This sort of thing is unbelievably difficult to hear. That is why I say I had the gift of having a cousin with dyslexia. It was unfortunate that my cousin had to go through it, but it taught me there was no way anyone can tell me a seven year old who can get an A doesn't want to get an A. That doesn't happen. It would be like saying you can please your parents, but you just don't want to. It doesn't happen that way. If they can, they will. If they can't, something is wrong. Even so, I hear it all the time, and that somehow I'm not doing enough. My in-laws are beautiful people who believe in us as parents, but they still don't understand that I cannot sit for ten hours and force my son to do something that he's not capable of doing. He is brilliant in his own way and can do the work, but finding the path to get there is a completely different thing.

I think most people still believe that LD is somehow caused by parenting. They may not admit it openly, but they think it. I can't really say my in-laws fall into this group. They know the problem is there and they've seen Peter's progression. Once he got to the Craig school, he went from not learning anything at all in four years to gaining those four years in a year and a half. He's almost at a level with others his age. So they've seen that. In the past, he couldn't write thank you cards. I would have to spell it all out for him. They gave him some money for a graduation present and he wrote them a long letter explaining what he did with it. It's barely legible. The dysgraphia and the dyslexia hold him back. The ideas were all there – the fact that he appreciated the gift and that he loves them…all that was there, even though it wasn't perfect. Two years ago he couldn't have put two sentences together on paper, but if you gave him a recorder he could tell you an entire story.

As far as stigma goes, I think we can talk about it terms of labels. The way I look at it is this: Peter is who he is. And you talk about labels! Peter is a food-allergic, dyslexic, dysgraphic, ADHD boy. He's also one of the most handsome kids I've ever seen. He has gorgeous blue eyes. He sees the world in different ways and I love when he tells me about it. He can fix any toy and he's very mechanically inclined. Those are all labels too. He is all those things. I do not mind him having the LD labels because if he doesn't know them, he can't overcome them. I have hopes he will one day go to college, and if I don't start telling him now, "You're dyslexic and you need to figure out what it affects the most, what's holding you back, what helps you, and why you are suddenly learning when you couldn't before, and you need to figure all this out for yourself before you get to college."

The fact is, I like who Peter is, and I like him just the way he is. I don't want him to be someone else. He's Peter. He's perfect. But he is different, and he accepts that about himself. He's unique that way. I'm not sure if I helped him with that or not. I probably did. As soon as the teacher started saying he wasn't trying and that he needs to work harder, I rebelled. I knew a child can't spend over six hours a day in school and then do over four hours of homework and then have everyone tell you that you're not doing enough. I started telling him they didn't know how he worked and that we would find someone who did know. And we kept trying. I threw away money on brain exercises and eye exercises and stimulate this and stimulate that – we did all that and then I'd say, OK we tried it and that's not how your brain works. And he's fine with that. He knows he's smart. He wants to figure it out himself.

I'm a firm believer that everybody has a place in this world. I think that's the hardest thing for people to accept and understand. When all your kids are in general education and have it easy, it's hard to realize that the ones who aren't perfect belong there too. Every child with LD learns differently. It's very difficult to say they learn, but most do eventually learn. They are not on the outskirts. They are right there with everybody. They *all* belong.

Marla

I have two children, a girl named Karen and a boy named Josh. When it comes to stigma, I would say it is much worse in public school. My daughter had a very difficult time with other children. Some of them were bullies.

One time, about a month after school started, Karen was standing in a line. All of a sudden the boys started teasing her while I was still right there. One of the boys turned around and asked her, "What is two plus zero?" She has dyscalculia and has a difficult time with math, and they obviously knew that. She didn't answer. Another boy asked her another question. Again, I was standing there but I thought I should try to let her handle it. But then she started crying and I wanted to scream at those boys. I eventually had to step in and stop it, but it continued from there.

Social skills were a difficult issue, especially since the town we lived in is particularly competitive. The culture is all about where you go to school, and who went to Ivy League, and who runs what company, and that kind of thing. I had lived there for years but I don't think I really knew all that was going on. I think my daughter Karen would have experienced a lot less bullying if we had moved to a calmer town, meaning a little more diverse, a little more inclusive.

I'm sorry to say that many of the problems come from the attitudes of the other mothers of the kids in the public school. They're so intense and the kids emulate that, even at a very young age. When Karen was in pre-school, it was fine, but when she went to public school things started to go wrong. There were always kids who could just tell that she was different, even though it wasn't that obvious. She doesn't have a social skills disorder, per se, but she was just so naïve and so vulnerable that they made things very difficult for her. I still can't think about it without getting tense and angry.

On the playground, the other kids would make up games and give the directions really fast. She has auditory processing problems and they were made-up directions, they weren't familiar at all, and they would talk too fast. She was the only one who couldn't understand. It really made her stand out. It was embarrassing for her. This happened all through kindergarten, first grade, second grade, all the way to fourth grade...I could not believe the level of bullying that went on. It was so intense. She was aware of it. She understood that she was getting bullied. It was really difficult for her. She was limping along with her LD but the primary reason we pulled her from public school was because of the social bullying. We just couldn't let it continue. It was damaging her so badly and we couldn't stop it. We tried, but talking to the other parents was like banging your head against a wall.

Things are so much better for Karen now. Enrolling her in a special school changed her life because she found kids who accepted her. She can be very quirky and say funny things, and kids here at this school are okay with that. They'll check her if she goes too far over the line. But she knows how to both fit in and stand out here. In some ways, Karen is "different" on purpose. She accepts her own differences and understands them better. She is truly a free spirit. She embraces popular culture, but at the same time, she wants to be who she is and follow a different drummer. She knows there is risk involved, but she knows it is safe here and that if she's a little different it is something to be celebrated and not frowned upon. It will be interesting to see how she reconciles all that as she gets older. We support her in being herself, but we caution her that there is a risk. We've been doing that since she was six, but there has been negotiation. It's a process. She has had difficulties at times. Girls are tough. All the mean stuff that is there in normal circumstances goes through the roof when girls with LD are mixed together with girls without LD. I haven't figured it all out yet, but we're taking it all one day at a time. Overall I would say, it is a joy and a journey.

Now with my son Josh, it's a little different. We pulled him out of the mainstream school because he needed it academically. Socially he was fine, but there was no program in place to tell if he was dyslexic so they started pulling him out of class and into special ed for everything, except for a few minutes of science – but how much science do you have in first grade? He was going back and forth every twenty minutes from the main classroom to the resource room and he hated it. The best thing I ever did was get him out of there. We were in hell. Everything was sliding downhill. My husband thought we were going to have to home school. My daughter was falling apart. I finally said to my six year old son, "Josh, you are smart. The school doesn't know how to teach you. They're not bad people. They care about you, but they don't know what to do. They don't know how to teach you the way you need to learn." The next day, he said to me, "It's not me – it's them," and then he told me that he told the teachers they didn't know how to teach him. My first thought was, 'Oh no!' but then I thought, 'Oh, who the hell cares?' A lot can happen in twenty-four hours, and maybe it just needed to be said.

That incident propelled me into bringing both my children to Craig School. There are people here who know how to celebrate the child and know how they need to learn. As a mother, the biggest stigma I have faced is my kids' fighting with themselves over who they are and accepting who they are. I don't know if this is specific to my family or this is more general, but my daughter is a teenage girl and things come up, challenges about self-perception and things like that – though all teens do that to some extent. I work all year round and this past summer my daughter went around to different places so she could interview for volunteer positions. She did that on her own. She volunteered a couple of times a week at an Arboretum, and she got so much positive feedback from this. I went to pick her up recently and I watched her with the kids at the volunteer program and she was so wonderful with them. I wasn't surprised, but I was so proud.

She has learned to push forward. She's fiercely independent, more so than I am ready for her to be. She thinks she's older than she is sometimes, in terms of wanting certain experiences, but this is self-advocacy and it is independence. This came after years and years of tutoring and role-modeling. And now that she's been helped by those things, she can have the later part of her day free after school and still have the time and energy to pursue her passions, or find new passions. She can breathe! That is the greatest gift, for her to have the space to figure out who she is and become that person.

STIGMA CANNOT SURVIVE
SELF-ADVOCACY

A Conversation with Cecilia Dintino, Psy.D

B efore we leave our visit with mothers of younger children who have LD and related disorders, I would like to share the insights of someone who has her feet in two worlds; one as a parent of a child with special needs and the other as a professional who must deal with the real-time affects of stigma on her patients, most of whom suffer mental illness.

Cecilia Dintino, Psy.D., is a clinical psychologist and the mother of a twelve year old son with special needs named Bernardo. This is her story, in her own words:

Cecilia

I work primarily with adults with depression, personality disorder, and anxiety. In addition to being a psychologist, I am also a drama therapist. They are two separate things, though in my practice I overlap them. I teach drama therapy at New York University where we use theater and different drama techniques and performance as a therapeutic agent.

Most of my clients do not have special needs such as LD or autism or related neurological disorders, but recently I've been working a lot with borderline personality disorder and I have seen more and more that there seems to be a cognitive piece involved. For instance, they can't always grasp the complexity of situations so they rely on oversimplified emotions.

In some of these cases, I would not be surprised to discover there were undiagnosed learning disabilities involved. We already know that many disorders and disabilities cross over. When you know someone with learning disabilities and see they also have symptoms of autism or Aspergers syndrome, you suspect they have some of these disorders too. For instance, severe ADHD can cause so many other problems in life that the person ends up with additional issues such as anxiety or depression. I really believe that for most of my clients, there was a special needs issue back in childhood that went unnoticed. It is what their entire personality has been formed around. I really appreciate and I think I understand this better because of my experience with my son Bernardo.

I see the impact of the effects of stigma on my clients all the time. It is such a problem. Let me rephrase that: it is *the* problem, and it is reinforced by the mental health system and by educational systems. There are efforts to decrease it by declaring that societal norms dictate how we view the disabled and if we change the norms it will help, but that is an extraordinarily difficult thing to do. I am aware of it in this way: the act of coming to treatment as a client and sitting with a therapist further entrenches the sense of stigma. It sets up a dynamic where the client is a person who has a problem and needs help and the therapist is the person without the problem. I've worked in group therapy and individual therapy and they talk about this a lot. They'll say things like "Oh, I guess now I've joined the crazy ranks." You walk onto a certain floor in a certain building and there it is: you have declared yourself as a person needing therapy and the stigma is there. Thankfully, that is beginning to change. People are speaking out about having mental illness or having a learning disability, but very real challenges remain.

I would also say there can be a silver lining in all this because, for some, it can be a relief to receive a diagnosis. It says, 'You are not a bad person. You have this real problem. You can get medicine and this is the kind of treatment that helps, and these are the tendencies that come with it.' Discovering all that can be a huge relief. Even so, there is a lingering stigma, especially when it comes to mental illness, and stigma has a way of eroding the identity of the person who has the problem. Their issue or problem becomes a part of their identity, so they not only have a form of mental illness or a disability, but they also have a sense of being stigmatized. In a way they stigmatize themselves and this becomes as great a burden as the stigma from others.

I believe the only way to not have stigma is to speak about it. It's like shame. If you keep it a secret, the shame increases.

Some people with mental illness recoil from the label 'mental illness'. It's the same for some with learning disabilities. They recoil from the word disability. The trouble is, many people need to accept those words if they hope to get services. I'll use anxiety as an example. A lot of my college students who have debilitating anxiety need to use the disability services. They absolutely need those services, so they have to declare they have a disability. They have to *own* the disability label in order to get the services they need.

I truly do understand the reluctance to accept a label, and I can speak about this as a parent too. There is a feeling that you want services for your child and then you get upset that your child is qualifying for the services. You're angry at the institution because you need them. It sounds ridiculous but it's true.

Being a therapist has not shielded me at all from the feelings common to parents of a child with special needs.

In my experience as a mother, I see and understand that parents want to talk about issues such as stigma and the effects of stigma on their lives and the lives of their children. When my husband and I go to PTA meetings and people start to talk about their child, sometimes they are sobbing. There is such a hunger to talk to people who will understand. Having a child with special needs can be lonely for a lot of parents, with enormous feelings of isolation. They don't know how to talk about it with people who don't understand the issue, and the reality is that many, if not most, people simply do not understand. They try to understand and they think they do, but they don't.

Bernardo

My son Bernardo was perfectly healthy in the beginning. I adopted him when he was six months old. He was healthy, very alert and engaged. Later, I began to notice he wasn't talking. He made up his own sign language. He would make gestures if he wanted to eat or go in the car, and he did it so well that it was difficult to notice that he wasn't talking. I had adopted him from Guatemala so I initially thought the problem was that he was bilingual. When I had him assessed, his comprehension for Spanish was fluent. Because of that, we held off for a bit and took a wait and see attitude. When he was a little older and I thought he should be talking, I brought him to a pediatrician, but it did not go well. He was crying and pushing her away and she said, 'There's something wrong with him.' Of course, I got very defensive. 'He's not talking at all?' she asked in what I thought sounded like an accusatory way. Before I could answer, she said, 'I can't further assess him if he doesn't quiet down,' and I left the office. I then found another pediatrician who had a different manner. Bernardo engaged with her with no problem, but even so, she suggested we have him assessed for speech therapy. I resisted and thought she was wrong. I was in denial.

Being a therapist had no bearing at all on my ability to accept her suggestions. Being a therapist and being a parent truly are separate identities. You might think that would not be the case, but my professional self and my personal self are completely separate. I'm really trying to bring them together a little more, but it's difficult. When the pediatrician suggested speech therapy, part of me thought, 'Oh that can't be, not *my* child.'

It's similar to the stubborn belief that a disability is somehow the mother's fault. I don't believe that for an instant. I really don't. Almost any diagnosis you show me, I say it's biological. I don't believe it's because the parents did something or didn't do something. I get outraged about it and yet I still get that about my son.

It comes in an accusatory tone as if my actions or inactions are to blame for my son's disabilities. Otherwise intelligent people still ask me I've ever considered reading to him, as if I never would have considered doing that. What they're really saying is, 'If you had only read to him, he wouldn't have these problems.' It's unbelievable.

I resisted the speech therapy at first, but mostly inside. I didn't actually refuse it, but I didn't like it, even after I agreed to have a speech therapist assess him. My husband Joe was there. We watched the assessment together. It was so clear that Bernardo couldn't say words but it also became clear that he couldn't follow directions. I remember my husband went into the other room and started crying. I kept insisting, 'No, this is just a transition phase because he's adopted.' There was some denial there. It was really difficult for me, especially because I still didn't suspect anything might truly be wrong. Again, I had noticed he wasn't speaking but I really did think it was only a developmental issue. When I think back on it now, it's really strange because there were other things too but I just didn't see them. Or if I saw them, I didn't understand what they meant. He was also hyperactive. He was driving us crazy at times. He jumped on furniture, he fell down, he had bruises all the time. There was no sitting still.

At the time I thought it was normal. I told myself, 'well, he's a boy, he's an energetic kid.' And I also took into account that he had an early start in a Spanish-speaking country and I attributed his language issues to that. This brings up another criticism that drove me crazy. People would tell me I shouldn't have a Spanish-speaking babysitter. They said that was the problem. I had friends who had bi-lingual children with no problems at all and some of those very same people told me that my son had problems because he had a Spanish-speaking babysitter. The fact is, I purposely chose her so he would have his Spanish along with English. Eventually I began to notice the people I knew who had also adopted children from Guatemala also had Spanish-speaking babysitters and those children were speaking with no trouble. Because of that, I believed for a long time that it was simply a delay in development. I held onto that for quite a while, but then the speech therapy came along.

Eventually the speech therapists began to tell me he had attention issues too. This became more pronounced when he got a little older and I had to take him to a clinic. He was about four or five then. They had a very hard time with him. They called him 'self-directed' because they couldn't get him to focus on what they wanted him to do. You would see them later, worn out from their twenty-minute session with him.

We weren't making a lot a progress but things got really devastating when I got him into pre-K at PS 3 in Manhattan. It's a school in the West Village, very creative, with a lot of artists. The very first day the teacher of the pre-K pulled me aside and said, 'We need help here.' At the time she, too, was saying it was simply a delay in development. She told me he was a year or a year and half behind the other kids. She then told me he qualified for SEIT services, or Special Education Itinerant Teacher services. This was someone who provided one-on-one help in the classroom. I remember crying when she told me that and I remember the other mothers trying to comfort me. The teacher was holding me and saying, 'Don't worry, I'm going to help you.' Just thinking about it now makes me feel like crying all over again.

Eventually Bernardo was diagnosed as having ADHD and mild Intellectual Disability based on his IQ score. His difficulties are so intense in the language-based area that the testing produces a very low IQ.

The Experience of Stigma

As far as stigma goes, I think it gets worse as the child gets older but it is still there even in the early years. When Bernardo finished pre-K, the teacher wouldn't graduate him to kindergarten. She said there was no way he could do it. Luckily, they instituted a 12 to 1 to 1 special education class in kindergarten that year. This means there are twelve kids to each teacher and a special ed teacher. It was the first such class, so he was going to be one of the first students. It would be the first time special education would come into our lives, but that doesn't mean there wasn't stigma before that. I remember going to a birthday party soon after I was told he needed speech therapy, and I remember feeling the stigma. The other kids didn't want to play with Bernardo. I also felt that the other mothers didn't want to be with me. Maybe they feared I might suggest a play date with their child and my son.

It may have been that my perception of his behavior had changed after his diagnosis.

Before the diagnosis, I probably thought he was just running around because he was energetic, but after the diagnosis you start to see things in a different light. You now see a group of kids kicking around a ball and you see your child off to the side. Bernardo learned very quickly not to participate. That's his problem now. He has anxiety about joining a group. Back then, he was either just sitting on the sidelines, which would break my heart, or he would engage in a way that I could see the other kids found annoying. We tried everything. We tried Little League and other sports, but he didn't like it and never wanted to go back. And you feel bad about it because you know much of this is all wrapped up in your own ego. You're of two different minds about it. One is saying 'This is my child and everything is fine,' while the other says, 'Oh my God, this is awful, this is mortifying.'

I wish I could say this wasn't true, but the fact is there are times when I've been embarrassed by my son's behavior. I would be surprised if most other parents couldn't relate to this. You feel horrible about it, but yes. It's there. You're still holding onto this idea that everything will work out fine. When he started going to a special education school, I would go to a Christmas concert and I would think all the other kids looked so impaired. You hold on to the possibility that he's not as bad as the others. You do that to try to get above the stigma. And then I would watch his performance and see that he was more impaired than the others. It was so hard.

He couldn't qualify to be mainstreamed and he was only five when he started the 12 to 1 to 1 class. On the very first day there was only one other student, who was this great big kid who was about five years older. He was about ten, but to my mind he looked like a teenager. It was just the two of them in there. I was crying and there was a friend sitting outside the classroom with me, and I was saying, 'I'm getting him out of there.' Eventually, this other boy turned out to be one of his best friends.

You would think because of my profession and training there would be a part of me that observes myself experiencing all this, but honestly, when it is so close you really don't see it. I have many clients who have children with special needs and when I work with them, I hear myself in what they are saying. I understand their feelings and I can help them and talk about it with them, but when I go home, I have as many issues as they do. I often have exactly the same issues they do, and I handle them just as well or badly as they do. Again, it's that fake dichotomy that says a therapist has more wisdom. You may be able to do the work, you know what to do and say, and know how to be an effective therapist, but none of that means you can always live your own life in a better way than they can. Life hits you the same way as it does your clients.

This can be a problem for some professionals, especially those who buy into the idea that because they have some particular expertise, it means they are not broken. If they do buy into it, they are going to get toppled at some point in a big way. I really accept the notion that I am as blind and as broken as the person I am trying to help, while at the same time, I am also really trying to help them. I believe having a child with special needs helped me to look at it this way.

None of us is spared any pain when it comes to having a child with special needs. Nothing protects us. Training and expertise are not a shield. When your own child faces stigma, it is very difficult to handle...especially when they are aware of it. Bernardo is sometimes aware of it and it breaks my heart. I keep trying to figure out how to help, but it's very hard to communicate with him about it. He recently did this play with other people who have disabilities and on the way home he said things like, 'I understand them, Mom. We have kids like that in my class.' He's in another theater group out on Long Island and sometimes he has anxieties because he doesn't want to go. He says they'll be reading from a script and he can't read. It turned out that's exactly what happened: they did start reading from a script and I saw him start to sulk in the corner. When I went over to get him, he said in a little sad voice, 'I just can't read'. So yes, he definitely feels it.

He has a sense that he can't do certain things. Things like baseball were just too confusing for him. He couldn't understand the rules. Some kids also made fun of the way he spoke. I made friends with some of the mothers of the students in his school. We would go on playdates together. He told me some of those kids called him a retard. Of course, when some of the mothers heard of it, they would apologize. Others would not apologize. I could feel their disapproval of Bernardo. I lived in Greenwich Village at the time, and there was a lot of diversity. But still, even in a diverse and tolerant place, the stigma was there. And why is that?

I think it is a general trend. There is so much pressure in our society that says everyone is supposed to be working, and the fact is, there are some people who simply cannot work. We are becoming a society that has no room for tolerance. And forget having a disability. There is so much pressure on people that even some who have no disabilities at all can barely function. The strength of a society comes from how we treat the weakest among us. We call disabilities a 'flaw'. Well, why is it a flaw? Because they can't make money? For some, that's what it all boils down to. They can't make money. Jean Vanier, the founder of the L'Arche communities, tells a story of a woman with severe disabilities but who was also extremely happy. She would run into a room and hug everyone, and one time after she left, a man in the room shook his head and said, 'what a shame.'

That man couldn't see that she was happy even with the evidence right before him. He missed the entire point.

Stigma as a Parent

I've also been at the receiving end of stigma as a parent. I have been directly blamed for Bernardo's disabilities. It's the same as the people suggesting he has troubles because I never read to him. I get things like that a lot. I have even gotten it from some family members. They'll say that Joe and I let him walk all over us or that we don't discipline him. The attitude that irritates me the most is when people will say, 'Well, what *we* do is…' and then they tell me how they handled their perfect child who has no disabilities. The implication is that the child is perfect because of 'what *we* do.' I always want to say, 'It has nothing to do with what *you* do.'

And that whole reading thing – it drives me crazy. Again, do you *really* think it never occurred to me to read to my child? A lot of people seem to think they taught their child to read because they read books to them. Therefore, they hint that Bernardo has trouble reading because his parents never bothered to take the time to read to him. They just don't understand. I've read to him countless times. I've taken him to so many reading programs and hired reading tutors outside of school, and it's always the same thing. He has trouble reading and people don't understand.

People are too quick to judge. I also think our culture is very anti-children in many ways. Children have so much pressure on them now. As a society, we want everyone to be perfect. This leads to stigma too. I have a sense that people don't accept differences and imperfections. I believe there are some who might not want Bernardo to play with their child because he might somehow infect their child with special needs. They want their child to be with others who lead them forward – not someone who might pull them down.

The other thing that comes up a lot with Bernardo is that he has ADHD so he has trouble waiting his turn and interrupts people…and that last one also gets to me. I get embarrassed. And I make gestures behind him to let the other people know he has problems, and I feel terrible about that. I really do. Sometimes I'll do it right in front of him. I'll say, 'Bernardo has attention problems and he has a little trouble'. I'll do that when I see people getting annoyed with him or looking at me as if to say, 'What's wrong with this kid?'

Once I do that, some people are completely fine with it. And, of course, there are some who start to tell me what I should do about it. A lot of people will tell me the diagnosis of ADHD isn't real. They'll say it's too much sugar and they'll start to look at what he's eating.

Some people say it's easier to have a child with physical disabilities because you get the looks right up front, but I don't know. Recently we were at the Apple store and Bernardo was getting an iPad. The salesman said, "OK, Bernardo, we're going to set you up here. Just read these terms of agreement and I'll be right back." I saw Bernardo panic and I was right there in a flash saying, "Oh, that's okay, we'll read it for you." I'm always stepping in. He's really into music now. He's taken drum, piano and now he just started bass guitar, and of course, I had to pop my head into the classroom and say, 'You know he can't read, right?' The teacher said, 'I already heard, we're ok with it.' But there's always that moment when he is asked to read and he can't do it, and it's just such a horrible moment for him. It's so awful. And I know I need to stop doing that because he's really starting to read. I need to shut up and let him try it.

It's important to step back a little because there sometimes comes a point when a parent has trouble accepting that their child can do more than they think that child can do. Parents do that all the time. I sometimes feel tension between Bernardo and me when I'm trying to figure out when to step in and when not. I can sense the moment he feels a little bit of anxiety and he can feel the moment I think he's not doing something right. It's so hard to figure out the right thing to do.

Another thing involving stigma is this: even in those nice supportive groups, it is incredibly hard to talk about how much you screw up as a parent when you have a child with special needs. What do I mean by screw up? Losing your temper. Losing your patience. Saying things you shouldn't. We all do it. It's so mortifying to admit you can get so angry, and that is really hard to talk about. We all know the stigma of being a bad, abusive parent is one of the worst stigmas of all. It's a horrible thing. I remember I had a student who had two children with disabilities. She told me some of the things she did as a parent and I remember thinking, 'Oh, that's awful'. And now my husband and I do the same thing. But that is the stigma. You're so afraid to talk about how angry your child makes you, or how you might sometimes be disappointed in your child. You love them like crazy and they please you so much sometimes…and see? See what I did just now? I feel I have to say I love him like crazy and that he pleases me sometimes, even though I'm sure people already know that. I still feel like I have to say that. But there is no place to talk about those things. It can even be difficult and painful to talk about it with your own spouse, even though both know the situation. What often happens at home is that you take turns being the bad parent. One day my husband might be the one who is the tough one and I suddenly become the all-knowing, warm mother. And then he does the same with me on those days when I'm losing it. Sometimes we can't talk about it between ourselves, so even there we find a barrier to being honest.

We don't live in a culture that allows for these feelings. In many ways, it's wonderful. We are very protective of our children. And it's true: my son shouldn't have to deal with me losing my temper. He shouldn't have to deal with that, but sometimes it happens. Sometimes he is so resistant and so difficult and you try and try, but there are those times when it gets to you. It rarely happens in any other area of my life. One of the reasons I'm a therapist is I'm extraordinarily tolerant of chaos. My clients call me in the middle of the night with a crisis and I can tolerate it. I can handle nearly any situation like that. But something unexpected has come up since I've had this child. I see a side of me I didn't realize was there. There are a couple of people who allow me to talk about those things, but not many. My clients come in needing to talk about these things too, and then they all have all this fear that I'm going to report them to the police.

It's a very tough situation. It's very, very difficult to say to anyone that you are embarrassed or infuriated by your disabled child.

In spite of all I've said, and my own challenges with stigma, I do think there are ways people can navigate through life even with something that may cause stigma. I believe the most powerful agent for helping is community support. In our case, it came in the form of doing a play with Bernardo and other kids with special needs. I realized it was a perfect model for every parent who has a child with a disability. It doesn't have to be a play, but it should be something that brings people together to talk. Whatever it is, it ends up being a shared community in which people are free to be open about having a child with a disability, and the child with the disability is also allowed to be open about it. And again, it doesn't matter what it is. If they like sports, it could be sports. It could be an art class. It could be a play.

It doesn't really matter. What matters is the support for both parent and child.

Some of my clients who have a child with special needs go to a similar support program. Being with other mothers who have children with special needs seems to be the thing that helps parents the most, along with being some kind of activist in some way.

As for Bernardo and how I help him deal with stigma, I believe there are three important things.

First, he needs to be empowered by knowing his situation and understanding his disabilities.

Second, he has to know how to advocate for himself.

Third, he needs to have a support network to allow him to do that.

I have a niece who has LD. Her disabilities are not at all as severe as Bernardo's, but she still gets stigmatized. She had a job but it didn't work out. People pick up on the fact that she has LD and it's hard for her. She got through college because she really utilized the services they have and she really advocated for herself, and now she needs to figure out how to do that in the workplace. She gains so much strength when she advocates for herself and speaks about her learning disabilities. It's the same for everyone, no matter how severe the disability. As with shame, stigma cannot survive the ownership that comes with self-advocacy.

Anne Ford and John-Richard Thompson

THE SILENCE OF STIGMA

Young Adults and LD

What do I mean by that phrase: The Silence of Stigma? In a word: shame. I have learned that silence is an unavoidable companion when it comes to stigma. There is the silence of parents who do not tell friends or family members what is going on with their child. There is the silence of a phone not ringing, or the silence of a doorbell not pressed; the silence of no friend calling your child or coming over to visit. There is the silence of people who do not want to appear impolite by bringing up the subject of what might be "wrong" with your child, yet nonetheless express their concern or disapproval with a glance. Finally, there is the silence of the stigmatized themselves; those who retreat from the world and from friendship and from acknowledging the pain that has stalked them since childhood.

I mentioned in the introduction that finding people with disabilities who would talk to me about stigma was an unexpected challenge. I'd like to tell you a little about that challenge. I have had no trouble at all finding young adults with LD who will talk about school, family life, relationships with siblings, and so forth. But stigma? No.

The disinclination to talk about it falls into two separate categories.

The first category I think of as those who might want to talk about it, but cannot. I had lunch with one such person, a young woman with severe LD, and her mother. When I brought up the subject, I couldn't do it by using the word *stigma*. I tried, but she didn't understand the word. When I used more familiar (yet more uncomfortable) terms such as, "Did your friends at school ever make fun of you?" I could see her retreat into herself.

"Yeah," she said. "It was really bad."

When asked to elaborate, that was the end of it. "It was really bad," was the best she could do.

The second category is made up of those who can articulate their experience with stigma, but cannot bring themselves to do it. They come up with excuses. "Oh, I can't talk to you this week, can we try for next week?" and then next week comes and they say the same thing. I met one young man at a disabilities event and when I approached him, he said he would love to talk to me about his experiences with stigma and told me he had a lot to say. "It was really bad," he began (which gave me the idea he might belong more to the first category than the second), but then he went on to describe in broad terms what it was like for him in school and in his neighborhood. We set up a time to meet but a few hours before, he sent me an email to tell me that it was just too painful for him to revisit those stories. "I have moved on with my life," he told me, and of course, I respected that decision.

Indeed, *moving on with my life* in a healthy, self-accepting way is what I hope for every child and adult with LD when it comes to stigma.

As first-hand accounts of the ordeal of stigma were difficult to come by, I once again incorporated the mothers of these young adults into the story – and heaven knows, it is certainly *not* difficult to find a mother who wants to talk about their child's experiences. We will hear from one mother and her adult daughter in the following pages.

I eventually managed to find another young woman who has made great strides as a professional in the LD world. She has learning disabilities herself, and has faced stigma, but hers is also a story of achievement in spite of her setbacks.

I remain indebted to them all, parents and young adults, who took the plunge and entered difficult territory. I fully appreciate and understand how difficult it was for each of them and can only stress again (as I did to each one in person) how very much I appreciate their efforts: I fervently hope their experiences and stories will spark new insight for our readers, and guide them toward new ways of helping or thinking about stigma in the lives of their loved ones.

YOUR CHILD IS NOT THEIR LD

An Interview with Dana Buchman,
Fashion Designer and Founder of Promise Project

Fashion designer Dana Buchman was born and raised in Memphis, Tennessee. She graduated from Brown University and was a President's Fellow at the Rhode Island School of Design before earning an Advance Degree in Fashion at London's St. Martin's School of Art. In 1982, Dana joined Liz Claiborne with a design job in knitwear and eventually started her own collection under the Liz Claiborne Corporation. In 2011, the Dana Buchman brand was sold to Kohl's and Dana left the fashion industry. She is now Chair of the Promise Project, a nonprofit organization dedicated to helping underserved children with learning disabilities get the support they need to learn. She is also the author of the memoir *A Special Education: One Family's Journey Through the Maze of Learning Disabilities.*

Dana and I met when the National Center for Learning Disabilities honored her for her work with LD. Her daughter Charlotte was with her. When it came time to write this book on stigma, I thought it would be a wonderful idea to speak with both Dana and Charlotte about their experiences with the issue.

I met with Dana first at the Promise Project office in lower Manhattan and began by asking her to introduce herself.

"My name is Dana Buchman. I have been a fashion designer, but now I'm working full time in the non-profit LD world with the Promise Project. I'm also the mother of two adult daughters, Charlotte and Annie. Our older daughter Charlotte has learning disabilities."

"When reading your book, I discovered your journey with LD is similar to mine," I told her. "LD ended up taking over my life."

"Mine too," Dana said. "I found out slowly and painfully that a child's struggles affect the whole family. LD affects siblings and relationships with friends. It especially affects the mother, and it does it in so many ways you don't expect. It permeates everything, but not always in a bad way. I learned a lot through the experience of having a child who learns differently, but a lot of those lessons came painfully. One of the most painful lessons of all is stigma and how to deal with it – or *not* deal with it. It is an important topic for both parents and children. There is already enough of a struggle with learning and having the world seem overwhelming and unmanageable. To have the stigma plopped on top of it all is really difficult. In my experience, and what I have observed in others, is that stigma can come in many forms. There's the stigma where the parent feels embarrassed because they have a child who is considered odd. That can be embarrassing to the ego as well as distressing. Then there is the stigma of the world. That can't be controlled. Seeing stigma rain down upon my child is what I suffered from. I felt distressed every time it happened. Our family was very supportive, so there were no serious problems there. For me, my greatest difficulty with stigma was watching my daughter suffer and wondering what I could do to help. I'm a fixer. You can do what you can do, but some things you just can't fix."

"I was the same," I said. "I continually looked for answers, hoping my daughter's LD would be cured. It takes a long time to realize and accept that there is no cure and LD does not go away."

"That's right. After Charlotte went off to college and I had more free time, I started to think about how difficult it had been for me and I wondered about families who didn't have the luxury of a husband and education and resources. There are a million children in the New York City public school system. One in five has some kind of learning problem. That is a lot of children and a lot of parents. I started the Promise Project with a group of friends who also went through the same things I went through. One of them had a connection to Columbia University so we opened a clinic up there. We try to focus on younger children because you can have more impact. Nine years old is when it really shows up. There is so much demand. Our phone rings off the hook. School mental health programs and school psychologists refer students to us, and there is word of mouth among parents too."

"In what ways do you help?"

"We provide a full battery of neuropsychology testing and meet with the parents so they understand what the next steps are. We also have a team of education coordinators who help the parents go back to the school. These parents have to be the advocates and we teach them how to do that. We are now in the process of starting a research component. We feel that LD has got to be like autism, we've got to know what it is. We have a brain study going now and we're trying to fund a research center for learning disabilities."

"I've met quite a few parents who have dedicated their lives to LD, the way you have," I said. "I did too. I hoped to share the lessons I had learned with other parents."

"I did the same thing," Dana said. "I started the Promise Project because my own journey with LD was so difficult. Having a child with special needs changes you as a person. Speaking for myself, I felt like I was the only one in the whole world going through that particular experience. So little is known about LD from a scientific point of view, and it's rarely talked about even though one in five children has learning or attention issues. It's astounding. Charlotte was informally diagnosed when she was three years old and then had a full evaluation at five years old. At three, she wasn't in school yet so I couldn't compare her to anyone else. She was also my first child so, again, I couldn't compare. The clues came a little at a time, through drips and drabs, and it took me a while to realize something might be wrong."

It's Amazing to Realize How Much You Don't Know

"And how did that happen?" I asked.

"It started when I saw that she seemed different from the other kids in the neighborhood. She couldn't do things other kids were doing. She was slow to turn over. She didn't crawl for a long time.

She went from not crawling to walking, which I've since learned is a marker for a potential learning problem. She was slow to speak and we wondered if it was a physical thing."

"You said she was informally diagnosed at three."

"She was, but it was so vague," Dana said. "There was only an inkling that something was going on, and honestly, the diagnosis didn't help. There was nothing specific, nothing I could put my finger on. With physical illnesses like measles or mumps you know exactly what it is and what you can do about it, but LD is an umbrella term. It is so inexact. It's amazing to realize how much you don't know. The vague diagnosis added to the confusion over Charlotte being different from other children. It was quite unnerving."

"The term *learning disabilities* is used for such a vast range of disability," I said. "It makes everything so confusing and difficult. It is used to describe someone who has mild dyslexia or someone who has profound disabilities, and everything in between. To put them all in the same group makes things difficult to understand at times."

"And what works for some, doesn't work for others," Dana said. "It's frustrating and a very tricky thing. I've heard people call LD the 'Silent Epidemic' because the children who have it look perfectly normal and you don't realize the depths of the suffering. It's that way for the parents too. They often think they are the only ones going through this. I certainly did. So many of us don't talk to anyone and we suffer in silence."

"I did the same thing. I didn't tell my family, didn't tell my friends. I tried to handle it alone."

"I worked for Liz Claiborne for years," Dana said. "She was my mentor and friend. She was like my mother. When she read my book about my journey with Charlotte and LD, she told me she had no idea I had been through all that. It's astonishing. I had worked for her for twenty-five years and in all that time, I never once talked about it. Not once! I could have: Liz was a compassionate person and would have understood and sympathized, but I never shared my story with her."

"It's a strange thing, that reluctance to share our stories," I said. "I have met some people, usually fathers, who take it as a personal affront to their ego that their child is learning disabled. It's an embarrassment to them."

"I didn't suffer from that," Dana said. "I suffered from other issues, such as the fear and anxiety generated by my lack of understanding my daughter's learning disabilities."

"It is genuine, that fear," I said. "It is profound. I don't think anyone who hasn't been through it can really understand it."

"Exactly," Dana said. "I knew Char needed my help to succeed in school, to maintain her self esteem, and to make herself understood when words didn't come easily, but I never felt confident that I knew the best way to help her. I never had a clear handle on what it felt like to *be* her. No parent ever fully "knows" their child, but LD adds a layer of complexity and urgency to parenting that is difficult to manage. I had so many questions I couldn't answer. *Why* was it so hard for Char to read? *Why* did she hold herself back in social situations? *Why* doesn't she just do it (whatever "it" was at the moment.) In addition, because the way LD shows itself changes as the child grows and new challenges arise, my job as a mom kept changing. It was so stressful to keep on top of where Char needed my support. I reached out regularly to her support team for guidance and they gave me good advice (for example, at Char's special school they advised that parents should not help with their child's homework. They said to leave that to the school and that I should spend time with her in the evenings enjoying her as a person, celebrating what she was good at, and what she felt good about doing or talking about.)"

"Did you find this advice helpful?" I asked.

"Very helpful, but homework was only one of so many issues that Char struggled with. What was I supposed to do when she was in tears because she didn't have a clue what the math homework even meant – even when I wasn't helping her with it? Or how could I help when she told me she couldn't go out to get lunch like everyone else because she wasn't confident about handling money at the pizzeria?"

"The challenges seem to be endless, don't they?"

"They certainly do," Dana said. "As soon as we figured out a solution to the problem of lunch at the pizzeria by showing her how to use a pocket calculator, something else would pop up, such as trying to figure out change in a taxi (this was before the days of iPhones). LD continually reared its head and morphed into another monster – and it truly felt like a monster to me sometimes! It always kept me on edge, and that more than the stigma is what occupied my time. It's not that the stigma wasn't there, but I was so busy with the constantly-changing ramifications of LD that I didn't put it front and center of my attention. And yet, having said all that, I come back to the fact that I didn't talk about LD all that much to others because I didn't really understand it myself and couldn't always think of a way to bring it up."

"In some ways, that's a form of stigma too," I said.

"It is! It's so difficult to explain what, exactly, is going on when it comes to LD. I think it comes down to this: we are all very different and we learn in different ways. The school age years are the most difficult for everyone because kids are often forced to do things they are bad at or that they have no interest in. Once they get out of school and they find something they love, it gets better for them."

"Was your daughter mainstreamed?"

"No. We were lucky enough that some of the best special schools in the country are in New York City. Charlotte was able to attend some of those all the way through high school. We wanted her to go a college for students with LD, but she said she was done with special schools. She went to Franklin Pierce College, and luckily they had a strong support team. She went for four years, graduated, and got her Masters from Boston University in Social Work. Her LD was not cured, but one of her strengths is that she is so resilient. She has no trouble telling a teacher she needs help. She also has an innate spirit of stick-to-it, of perseverance. Those are some of her strengths, and it is so important to remember these kids' strengths."

"When you wrote about your upbringing and your personality, you said there was no tolerance for imperfection, vulnerability, no room for being human."

"That's a little hyperbole," Dana said, "but yes, that is essentially correct."

"Was that a challenge for you when it came to your daughter's LD? You have the personality you have and suddenly you're confronted with something that goes against that personality. Was there anger…?"

"Yes, there was some anger," Dana said. "I wrote about how my personality traits clashed with Charlotte's disability. For instance, it made me angry when she couldn't figure out how to dial the phone. I didn't understand it. I was so convinced that a person should be able to dial a phone – that *any* person should be able to dial a phone. In my own defense, the truth is I had never seen this before. I had never been exposed to somebody who couldn't do it. My lack of information and knowledge was a contributing factor to the suffering. I was a high achiever and ambitious, and suddenly I was faced with something I did not understand. I was not equipped for it. Fortunately, I had a passion for my daughter. We are lucky as mothers to have that innate passion for our children. That never wavered. Even so, there was a great deal of frustration and confusion."

"How old was she when she couldn't dial a phone? Six?"

"Around that age, maybe a little older. She was eventually able to do things like dialing the phone, though it took her longer to learn and she needed extra help. I think this sort of thing is why there is the debate between learning differences and learning disabilities."

"Which do you prefer?"

"I prefer 'disability' over 'difference.' I would have liked to favor 'difference' because it's softer than disability. It doesn't sound as final. But Charlotte pointed out to me that in a world where everybody learns one way and she learns another, it is a disability to learn differently."

"That's an interesting way of looking at it," I said.

"Maybe someday that will not be true, but for now it is."

Being Aware of a Struggle is a Strength

I asked Dana if she ever had trouble or was embarrassed when telling someone her child was going to a special school.

"No, that was never a problem for me," she said. "I know that stigma exists, but that wasn't one of mine. I was just so grateful they were there for her."

"Did you ever notice that you were treated differently by other mothers when they found out you had a child with LD?"

"No, but Charlotte was sometimes teased by other children who were not in a special school. There was a teenage boy who asked my other daughter, very loudly: 'Is your sister retarded?' That was awful. The image of that day is still fresh in my mind. It was terrible. I never felt embarrassed that she was in a special school but I felt distressed that she had to go through things like that, and that she was so isolated during her high school years. I think we parents also feel distress and disappointment because we bring our own experiences into it. I remembered how things were for me in high school and I knew she wouldn't get to do all that."

"Did Charlotte struggle with social issues?"

"Oh yes, she had a lot of difficulties socially. It made me sad to see her struggle that way. That can often come with learning disabilities, but who knew? I certainly didn't. Nobody tells you that."

"Another big issue with stigma is society in general," I said. "Society, or the public, still has expectations of people being a certain way. If you're not, it makes people a little uncomfortable. With learning disabilities, it can be even more pronounced. I don't know how it is for Charlotte, but for some with LD, there is no outward sign of a disability. Suddenly they may say something that makes no sense at all. At first people think they have heard incorrectly. It can cause a lot of problems."

"Absolutely," Dana said. "Charlotte doesn't do that, but one of her issues is expressive language. It takes her a few seconds to say what she wants to say. In a social group when everybody's talking fast, by the time she comes up with the thought and says it, the conversation has moved on."

"But she seems to have done well in college with a mainstream group."

"Yes, but she didn't have a lot of friends," Dana said. "She found her way. Her resilient side gives her the ability to be alone."

"Did she ever talk to you about any of this?"

"Oh yes. It wasn't like she thought everything was great all the time. She knew she had issues socially. We talked five times a week. I coached her."

"And how did you do that?" I asked.

"When I was coaching well, I did a lot of listening and validating her feelings," Dana said. "I made gentle suggestions beginning with the phrase, 'Did you think about trying this?' and I expressed my admiration for how hard she was trying, and how intuitive she was to pick up on her own social awkwardness. Just being aware of a struggle is a strength. It is also one to be acknowledged and praised. And of course, I always reminded Char of her incredible strengths and abilities, which de-emphasized the constant rumination – on both our parts—of the 'dis-abilities.'"

"Were there times when you felt you were not coaching well?" I asked.

"Yes. When I went into my 'fix it' mode, I was less effective. It isn't easy being a mom, and it took me a long time to realize that my zooming in to tell Char what to do was not the best way to be helpful. I imagine it feels intrusive and also perpetuates the sense of disability and the sense that the child needs to be instructed constantly. That's not a good message. In fact, I am still wrestling with this deep-seated urge to state the solution rather than express my confidence that Char can figure it out on her own. It works best if I just stand by and help her handle the emotions that social awkwardness brings up. Patience and compassion are the key things a parent should keep in mind (easy for me to say now!). I had to constantly remind myself that Char's mind works differently from mine and that my job was to listen and try to hear the subtext of what she was saying, to empathize with her pain and sorrow, to gently make suggestions (but not too many and not too forcefully); and to come back again and again to my confidence that she would be able to make her own way."

"And how has she done at making her own way?" I asked.

"She got extra help in college and, luckily, she knows how to use the help. She had a tutor and that tutor became a mentor and a friend. Her professors loved her because she's very responsible. She went to class every day, she tried to do her homework, and she didn't have a bad attitude. She's interested in learning and really enjoyed college."

Learning Disabilities: A Pop-Up

"Social skills can help lessen the effects of stigma," I said, "but that assumes the child has positive social skills. If they do not, their difficulties with social skills can help to create stigma."

"Socially, Charlotte learned to compensate and make a life for herself, like we all do."

"Does she still face stigma now and then?"

"She does, yes," Dana said. "She calls it a pop-up, in that you never know when it's going to pop up and bite you. Learning disabilities will suddenly appear wherever you are, often at unexpected times. It will highjack the conversation or a person's view of you. It is constantly there and sometimes it can be horrendous. She was taking a summer course at NYU and she was called on to read out loud in front of sixteen people. It was hard for her and she lost her place. The guy next to her pointed to his book to show her where it was. In that case, I think there was a bit of a self-imposed stigma. Everybody had to read a passage that day. She probably read hers more slowly and with difficulty but I don't think anyone took much notice of it."

"I think that once people with LD are used to having stigma in their lives, they assume it is always there," I said. "They go into situations anticipating that people are going to have certain feelings about them."

"This is exacerbated when they do not ask for help. Many of Charlotte's disabled classmates were not willing to ask for any help at all. They were embarrassed by it. Many of them would not use the services available."

"This is not uncommon," I said. "Students with LD have services all through grammar school and high school and then when they get to college, they refuse the help and end up with nothing but trouble."

"I also believe that some kids shouldn't go to college," Dana said. "Their skills and interests lie in other areas – and this goes for kids with LD and without. I am not completely convinced college was right for Charlotte. She was able to do it and I think she's proud of her accomplishments and she learned a lot, but I don't think college is for everyone."

"And she graduated?"

"Yes. She went on to get a Masters from Boston University in social work, though she did have a little trouble along the way. She has organizational issues and in her social work internship, she had to carry a file around and keep track of thirty-five children. It was a nightmare, the worst thing to ask her to do. One day her notebook exploded all over the school. The person running the program contacted BU and said Charlotte wasn't competent. The social worker program called her in and she was confronted with thirteen people telling her how she wasn't measuring up. It gives me chills just thinking about it. In response, she said, 'You advertise this as a strength-based program and that isn't what you are doing here.'"

"She advocated for herself."

"She did, yes. She learned to do that through the special schools she attended. In those schools, there were kids like her and there was a certain amount of acceptance. I wish that was the case overall, in every school, in every situation."

"It's pretty clear that you believe there is still a stigma associated with special needs."

"Oh yes! I believe there is a huge amount of stigma."

"It's in the family too," I said. "I think some parents just can't accept it and so they push the child into being something the child cannot be."

"Many parents are living through their kids," Dana said. "I guess we all do. I was doing that also."

"Fathers particularly seem to have trouble with this," I said. "It's undeniable that our audience is 95% mothers. I think a lot of it is a matter of ego. They didn't want to have a child who was disabled. Of course, not all fathers are like that. Not at all."

"My husband was fantastic," Dana said. "He spearheaded the whole thing. When we first noticed something wasn't quite right with Charlotte, he was the one who suggested we take her to the doctor to see what it was."

"It's a shame that some parents wait so long," I said. "I know a family where the young son obviously needed to attend a special school but the parents said, 'no, no, he's going to make it without that.' And, of course, he didn't. Eventually they gave in and he sent him to the school he needed and he's thriving. They had a fear of labeling."

"It breaks my heart that there are kids in public schools who haven't been diagnosed. It happens for a lot of different reasons. Sometimes it's due to flaws in the system. At Promise Project, we had a child who was being held back in third grade a couple of times so he ended up being twelve years old with all these nine year olds. Imagine the sense of stigma he felt!"

"Another problem is the cost of special school," I said. "They can be expensive."

"They can, but there are special schools within the public system. There are better things to do than nothing, and certainly the special education within the public schools is invaluable."

"There must also be a parent advocate involved," I said. "If there isn't, things sometimes don't get done. The school can help, but that parent advocate is the most important element."

"I had my own experience with that," Dana said. "When Charlotte was at a special school, she said to me one day, 'Mom, nobody knows you.' That was an eye-opener. I thought the schools were handling everything, and I therefore didn't need to get involved, but it's not true. You absolutely need to be involved. At another school, when I finally decided to get more involved, they said, 'We were waiting for you.'"

"The first special school I ever saw was the Gateway school," I said. "It was in a gymnasium then, with temporary walls to make the classrooms. It didn't look at all like the school I imagined for my child."

"Charlotte went to Gateway too," Dana said.

"The first time I saw it I thought I was going to die," I continued. "I cried so hard. I didn't think she belonged there. At that time, I didn't even know there was a real problem. She hadn't been formally diagnosed. It was such a shock."

"It's not easy being the mother of a child with special needs."

"And that is another question I have. Do you think it is worse for the child or for the parent?"

"Worse for the child. We're grownups. We've had our lives."

"I mean the sense of stigma."

"I still say the child. I have a lot of faults as a mother, but thankfully, I didn't have any ego problems over the fact that Charlotte had LD. My biggest issue and the one that was the worst of all for me was seeing her suffer."

"I asked that because I've often thought Allegra wasn't really aware of the stigma."

"Oh, I see what you mean."

"She wasn't always aware, but it tore me apart," I said. "I think I had it worse."

"I hadn't thought about it that way."

'Allegra often didn't even know there was a problem at all. She was lucky that way."

Dana said: "Charlotte knows."

"And that's the difference," I said. "That would be more difficult."

"You are in a position of seeing things differently than your daughter," Dana said.

"Yes. Allegra is unaware. I still get embarrassed when she says things that are off the wall."

"Part of that, in your defense, is that you're concerned about what others might think. Stigma is a complex thing. You're embarrassed because you're worried about your daughter."

"I agree," I said.

"A big source of difficulty was Charlotte's contemporaries, or her sister Annie's friends. They were all nice to her, but there were challenges with contemporaries who weren't in school with her. They didn't really understand her. She had trouble playing board games, for instance. She couldn't move a piece on a board to where it was supposed to go."

"Allegra had the very same problem."

"Who could have expected that to be an issue? The lack of information added to the struggle for me. I had no idea that my child wouldn't have been able to play a simple game like that. The lack of information and knowledge about LD is a huge problem for parents. It's a huge contributor to stigma. You see the kid do something odd and you just don't understand what is going on. In the schools, if the teacher is not familiar with LD, they will tell the kids they're lazy, bad or stupid. It's shocking that some teachers still don't know anything about LD."

"Stigma can also be caused by various people at various times in a child's life," I said. "It could be teachers, family members, friends – it all depends on the situation and time of life."

"Charlotte tends to withdraw from others and pull away if she perceives any form of stigma. I think it's a form of self-protection. She would keep to herself, even when she didn't want to. For instance, she might not join in playing a game because she feared she wouldn't be able to understand the rules. LD would invade her social life. She would anticipate that by holding back. I think a lot of kids do that. They're more reserved than they want to be."

"And now for the most important question of all," I said. "What advice would you give to parents who might be feeling stigma themselves or whose child is experiencing it? What would you say to someone who comes to you and says their child is being teased because of their learning disabilities?"

"The thing that most helped me was to focus on Charlotte's strengths," Dana said. "You have to pay attention to the struggles, of course, but you must always remember, and see, and enjoy, and appreciate the good. Really *pay attention* to your child's strengths. Stigma is a complex thing. It has so many facets. People learn so differently. You can have an artist who can barely read but is amazingly creative. There isn't much stigma in that case, but there might be for someone who can't read who is also not an artist. Look at Van Gogh. He wasn't a great reader at all. The arts attract people with LD. Charlotte loves art. We would do art projects together. She goes into her zone when she's doing her art. She relaxes.

She doesn't plan. It just comes out of her. It's amazing. We would make paper dolls for hours and her attention would never waver."

"Focusing on the positive and building self-esteem is key," I said. "It helps the child withstand the stigma."

"Yes. And you must always remember that your child is not their LD. There is a lot more. Your job as a parent is to keep in touch with everything that is there. You need to find the good. Try to enjoy all the different facets of your child. Your child will feel it."

HOW DO I HANDLE IT?
IT IS WHAT IT IS

Questions and Answers with Charlotte Farber

When I told Dana how challenging it was to find a young adult willing to talk about their experiences with LD and stigma, she suggested her daughter Charlotte Farber might be agree to be interviewed. As it turned out, her schedule did not allow her to come to our office. Instead, she agreed to be interviewed by her mother with questions supplied by me. I think this worked out for the best as Charlotte was more comfortable talking to her mother than to someone she had never met, especially on such a sensitive topic. I've come to realize that memories associated with stigma really do last long into adulthood – possibly for an entire lifetime. For some, speaking of these memories is reliving a form of trauma.

After Dana spoke to Charlotte and sent us her responses to our questions, Dana wrote to tell us what a difficult and painful experience it had been for her daughter. "Hi Anne," she wrote. "I sat with Charlotte this weekend and got a few answers. This is going to take some time. I could tell she found it quite painful to revisit school and college days as a young person with LD. Her whole body language was one of sadness, as if she had melted into the couch at the memory. Oh, this LD is a huge burden! It shows how important it is to write a book describing how devastating the stigma of LD can be to the psyche!"

I now present our questions to Charlotte and her responses, as told to her mother Dana Buchman.

Hi Charlotte. Thank you so much for agreeing to answer some of our questions. First, can you tell us a little about yourself?

My name is Charlotte Farber. I'm 30 years old. I went to elementary school and all the way through high school attending special schools in New York City. When I graduated I decided I was ready to continue my education in a mainstream environment and I went to Franklin Pierce University in Rindge, NH, where I got my BA in American studies. It was *very* different being in a mainstream school for the first time, but Franklin Pierce had a great student services center where students with LD could get help from very knowledgeable support people. I then went on to Boston University and got a Master of Social Work—who would have thought? Haha. Grad school was hard, also, but by then I had gotten really good at knowing how I learn and where I can get bogged down or go astray. And I was always comfortable asking for help—from the beginning, when I was quite young. That's one of my strengths. It's so important to be aware of your strengths, even more important than knowing what's difficult for you! I got my LCSW (social work license) and worked as a social worker in Boston for two years after my masters. I recently moved back to New York City to decide what I want to do next.

Can you tell us about the type of learning disability you have?

One from every column: dyslexia, dysgraphia, dyscalculia, executive function, expressive language issues, and ADD (not ADHD—hyperactive, I'm not!)

Our book is about stigma and how some people do not understand people with learning disabilities. Did you ever experience anything like that? Can you tell us about it?

Yes. I experienced it all my life. I went to art camp when I was in high school. I loved it but there were times when LD made itself known. I was in a jewelry class and the teacher asked me to measure something on a ruler. That was just impossible for me to do. I tried to explain it to the teacher but she was just annoyed that I couldn't get it. She didn't understand. I didn't say anything more to her but I ran out of the class, went back to my bunk, and cried my eyes out. Another time, I was in the weaving studio and the director of the art camp went up to the weaving instructor to tell her I had LD. She whispered it to her really loudly, right in front of the group, and I was standing there, too. I was so embarrassed. She was trying to be helpful. But she wasn't aware of the stigma of LD. It would have been better if she had pulled the teacher off to the side and said, "Charlotte has LD and has trouble with following instructions for threading the big loom. Can you try to accommodate her?"

A lot of young people with LD do not want to talk about it, or feel they need to hide it. Have you ever felt that way?

I went to special schools and it was ok to talk about LD there. Everyone had LD and it was comfortable to be in the open, but when I went to college, where even the teachers were not familiar with LD, it was really hard. When I explained that I had LD, some teachers were quite willing to work with me. Others wanted to be helpful, "Oh, you have LD?" but didn't know how to be helpful. When that happened it would set me back—I had gotten myself together to go up to them, found a time to speak to them in private, but I was reminded once again that telling them wasn't enough. The fact is, most people don't understand LD. They have no idea what learning disabilities are. To them, a kid with LD looks like a "normal learning" kid. So people can't see it. LD is invisible. In a way, this is a good thing but can also make it harder. So why don't young people want to talk about it? It is painful. It's embarrassing. No one wants to relive past frustrations. Actually, current frustrations, too: people with LD still experience frustrations every day.

They may also feel a sense of the unjustness—why do I have to have LD and you don't? Also, sometimes people with LD don't know how to talk about it. I know that I don't want to talk about LD when I'm with people who I know will have no idea what it is.

Also, I have all these emotions around it—a lifetime of emotions—and sometimes I just don't want to bring it up. Also, I don't want people to think that's what I am. If I mention I have LD, will they always think "LD" when they see me? I am a lot more than LD. So sometimes (most times) I don't mention it.

How do most people react if you tell them you have learning disabilities? Are they understanding? Are they confused?

They may be understanding. Or they may not know what LD is. It depends on who you are talking to. Mostly they don't care either way, probably because they have never felt what it is like to live with LD. In their mind, they may know what LD is, but they often want to move onto another topic.

I have a friend from Japan. I once told him that there are certain things I have challenges in and sometimes I need help with those. For instance, in math. He just said, "Use a calculator," and changed the subject. He's right that a calculator is sometimes a good solution, but he wasn't interested in learning more about what it feels like to have to rely on that.

Do you have any thoughts on LD when it comes to jobs and the workplace?

Schools sometimes help you with your LD, but in the job market you're on your own. There's no one to help you figure out when (and if) you should describe what LD you have. You don't want to scare the boss, or the company, by making it look like you can't do the job. On the other hand, I've even heard of "tokenism", where a workplace might hire you because having someone with LD gives them diversity. Can you imagine?!

You don't have to tell someone during an interview process that you have LD. You wait until after you've been hired.

If I tell a boss about LD, he might say, "OK. What do you need?" But a boss doesn't have time to sit with you and help you figure out what you need to succeed at the job. You have to do that. If you go to the boss to ask for an accommodation, you have to go in knowing already what you want. It's important that you understand your own learning style and challenges and be able to explain them in a way that people might be willing to listen to you. You want to be clear, accurate. But you don't want to come off as helpless. If you do you might not get or keep your job. And you're not helpless.

The bottom line is this: having LD can be very stressful. And how do I handle it? I think of it this way: it is what it is.

In your mother's book, you mentioned something called the "Charlotte tornado". Can you tell us what that is?

I was talking about my locker at school – the physical messiness. I used that term to give it some humor. Now that I'm older and have my own apartment it is a lot better. The "Charlotte tornado" still exists in my apartment from time to time, but I've learned how to handle it. When I see it getting out of control I take the time to organize it. It's hard but I know how important it is to keep order. And this is one of those things that gets better after high school: a locker is small, and you're trying to keep it neat with more stuff than will fit. And rushing between classes. Now that I am not in school and have a full apartment to store my things, it's much easier. But even at my job it's hard for me to organize my desk. I could use someone to help me—a coach or something. But there isn't anyone. So I hope a colleague can help me. Or I do it slowly by myself.

Do you prefer learning disabilities or learning differences?

The terms serve different purposes. Learning difference is relatively new. It fits into the neurodiversity movement which says there are different ways to be, but it doesn't capture the things you really have difficulty with—it glosses over them. Learning Difference feels better than Learning Disability. But you might not get the accommodations or funding you need if you say Difference and not Disability.

Disability is not empowering. It looks at what is going on from a problem perspective. But both terms can be useful. When I was eight, I couldn't read. I went to a program called Lindamood-Bell and now I can read—I changed my brain and went from not reading to reading. I would call my reading a learning *difference*.

With math I wasn't able to change my brain, and still have a hard time with numbers. I'll always have a math issue and I'd call it a learning *disability*. I have learned strategies so I can get around ok: I ask people. Or I use a calculator.

And I stay away from jobs or tasks that are numbers oriented. If you have a learning disability in math or whatever, you don't want to get into a situation where you're doing what you're not good at when, with a little attention, you can put yourself in situations where you are doing what you are good at!

What do you think of your mother's book A Special Education? Were you at all reluctant to have your story made public?

Not at all reluctant because it's a mother/daughter book. By telling my story I felt I was empowering myself. Taking away stigma by not hiding my LD. I've always felt ok with sharing something like this. I had the privilege of a supportive family and supportive schools.

There is a lot that I know now that I didn't know when we were working on the book. For example, the challenges of grad school, jobs and even relationships that I wasn't aware of. The challenges aren't so bad that you forget what's good in your life, but some were tough.

In grad school, the huge challenge was getting papers in on time. I had no road map for time management. Also, I went to a university where professors and administration had no awareness of LD—none at all—and there were no services available. On top of doing graduate level work, I really had to advocate for myself the whole time.

As far as difficulties at work go, I never had a job (except catering) during high school. When I got out of grad school and was looking for a job, I had to work hard to file accommodations requests and to know my rights. Even so, I risk getting fired if I don't meet the job requirements. It's a gray area.

You were a success in high school (Winston Churchill award) and you went through college, and got your Masters Degree, and you are continuing to work hard and succeed. Does LD still cause problems?

Yes. I still can't calculate tips. But now I use an app on my phone. I also still have trouble communicating verbally sometimes. I have to decide when to tell people, at a job interview, for example, that I have LD. The way I deal with it is, if it may come up in the job, I tell the interviewer, but I downplay my LD a bit. I minimize it. And I offer a solution at the same time that I bring up the issue: for example, my handwriting is not always clear (though I have to say it has gotten much better in recent years. Go figure!) so I tell them I will need to use a computer. Somehow I figure out how to get around it. Like anyone in an interview, I make it clear that I can do the job.

One of the things that made me sad as a mother was that my daughter had no friends. Did you have the same problem Allegra did with friends? How have you handled friendships?

I had social anxiety around making friends. I did have a few good friends but not tons. And I wasn't part of the big groups. I'm still not part of big groups. I guess I'm an introvert. I don't know if I was born this way or if there is a connection to LD.

Partly I avoid big groups as self protection so I don't have to be rejected—I can hide. You see these other people in those groups and making friends, and you try to figure out how you can fit in—it's like puzzle. My expressive language issue may play a part too. To socialize you have to think on your feet and be ready to respond to questions. It's like one of those hand games where you have to get the rhythm right—someone says something and you have to say something back at the right time, with right tone, and with the right facial expression. Part of my LD is to process things differently, at a slower pace. I do much better one on one than in a group setting.

What's good is that I know that now.

How are you now with your LD?

Answering these questions is hard. I am used to answering questions and thinking about my LD and what it's like to have it, but it's still hard to go into it. To do this, I'm revisiting painful experiences, which is something I'm not good at.

Since high school I've learned that if you focus so much on the negative you don't get to see what you're good at. Your world view is a different world view if you stay focused on what you have trouble with.

I still have LD. But it's now not my entire life and I know that. I can do just as well as other kids. When I was in school, my focus was, "I have a learning disability." Now the LD doesn't identify me but I am still different. But I can do things well—and sometimes even better than someone who doesn't have LD. Having had to struggle as I have has made me resilient, strong. I am able to persevere.

Do you have any advice for kids or young adults with LD who may be facing stigma in their lives?

I do have some advice. First of all, find someone close to who you can talk to about your life and your life with LD. Then you can have a deeper conversation with that person and feel supported. It's nice to have support when you're going through struggles as a young person, and especially so if there is LD on top of it. It helps not to feel you're facing the world all alone.

You might also find hobbies that you enjoy. You'll make a connection with other people that has nothing to do with your LD.

If you're an older teenager or young adult you could find other kids similar to you and start a support group. I never did that but I always wished I'd had one, especially after I finished school (at my special schools, all the kids around me had LD.) When I left there and went to mainstream college and afterwards, I was wishing I had somewhere to go where I could be with other kids with LD, like a club. At college they had a learning center but it was strictly for academics. This wouldn't be like that. It would be a support group run by and for people with LD to discuss the social, emotional and even practical side of having LD.

Unfortunately, I've never heard of such a group like that. I wonder if people with LD would go to such a support group. Most people I know with LD don't talk about it now. It's not something to talk about. Being in school with LD was a painful time—why go through it again? LD is no longer a main focus of our lives. We have found ways to build a life that isn't primarily focused on LD

I imagine this was another reason no one wanted to be quoted in this book: not just the stigma, though that is also big. But just reluctance to relive what was painful.

Do you have advice for their parents?

Be patient

Be collaborative

Don't be intrusive. Take cues from your kid about what they need. Stand by to help but don't be pushy. Discuss with them and with their school the best way to help. Sometimes it is important for the parent to intervene, especially with the school. For example, in third grade my parents scheduled a meeting with my math teacher when they felt I wasn't getting it. The teacher hadn't realized since I was so easy going. So their meeting with him was helpful.

The most important thing I would say is this: LD isn't the only thing to talk about with your teenager. There is a lot more to your kid than her LD!

HOPE MAY WAVER BUT LOVE ENDURES

Serena and Charles

Many of my readers have children in special education due to something like dyslexia or ADHD and they and their children bear some of the burdens of stigma. What happens when your child has more profound disabilities that may come with behavioral problems or cause troubles that, on the surface, have little to do with their disability, such as troubles with the law or troubles caused by their own emotional immaturity?

Stigma in these cases can be intense. It can result in actual shunning of the child or young adult, or sometimes the entire family.

"I don't want you playing over there," a mother might warn her child when talking about a neighbor with these types of disabilities. "He's unpredictable. He's dangerous."

What is it like for the mother of the "unpredictable" child? Is she truly aware of the stigma? Or has it become such a part of her family's experience that she no longer notices it?

I've known one such mother, Serena, for many years and I've known her only child, a son named Charles, since the day he was born.

I knew Serena's son had challenges but I did not know the extent of those challenges until I asked to speak with her about stigma. Hers is a difficult story, but I've never known her to complain or feel sorry for herself. She is a devoted and caring mother and an advocate for the disabled, and I am proud to call her my friend.

"I'm a little anxious to talk about all this," Serena began. "I know you are someone who understands all this, but even so, I'm really nervous."

"Why is that?" I asked.

"I guess it's because my kid is so messed up, and I'm just so used to the stigma that I don't talk about it very much. It's crazy. I know that you, personally, don't have any feelings of stigma with this, but even so, it's very upsetting to me. It's very personal. It has been such a big part of our lives for so long that you begin to think people aren't going to want to talk to you anymore once they find out about it. You also feel like no matter what you do, you still could have done something more. I think I have suppressed my feelings about stigma for so long that it makes it difficult to talk about them openly. In fact, I feel like I'm about to cry right now. I think I will be relieved after I talk to you...but it's just so difficult and it brings up many bad memories."

"Let's start with you and your son Charles," I said. "Tell me about him. Where is he now and how old is he?"

"He's now twenty-one and he's living at my parents' ranch. He can't get in any trouble there. As for me, I am basically a helicopter mother who is really having a hard time backing away. My son is now an adult and I'm having a hard time. As for Charles, his diagnosis is obviously not his entire self. We once had a doctor who told us that if he was schizophrenic, it would be a blessing because it could be controlled with medication. Our problem is that his issues are so unusual no one can really treat him. He's got Asperger Syndrome and he's got a mood disorder and he's got Klinefelter Syndrome, which means he has an extra X chromosome. There are different levels of this syndrome and I had no idea he was on the far end of the spectrum until he was in a study at Columbia University. When they interviewed him, I was told he was one of the worst cases they had seen. Klinefelter is only in boys. It makes them sterile and most men don't even know they have it until they go for fertility treatment. Most who have the syndrome will also have learning disabilities and major social skill problems. About 20% of them end up in jail because they don't have good judgment. They don't have a filter. They are slow to mature. Most of them will do absolutely anything to get friends because nobody wants to talk to them. That's one of the reasons why a lot of them go to jail. For instance, I know of one young man who was totally ostracized by his classmates. Two older guys befriended him and convinced him to go into houses and burglarize them. He was so desperate for friendship he would do whatever they asked. When they finally got caught, nothing happened to the two men who put him up to it, but the Klinefelter kid went to prison."

"Did you start noticing a problem with stigma early on?" I asked.

"Oh yes. One of the reasons we sold our first house in Oklahoma City was because the houses in that neighborhood are very close together. Our block was a pretty quiet block and all the kids on the street would play with each other. But not Charles. None of the other kids would play with him. When he was about five, we moved away because of those other kids and their parents."

"They would make fun of him?"

"All the time. We moved to an area where each house has a decent-sized lot. Our neighbor had a big wall around her house and I only met her twice in five years. On the other side was a family with two kids. They played with Charles in the beginning, mostly because we had a pool and they didn't. They backed away as soon as swimming season was over. In some ways, our isolation was something of a relief. We didn't have anyone else close by. We didn't have anyone looking at us. Nobody really knew who we were."

"You found that helpful?"

"Definitely. Even at a very young age, Charles would do things that no one else would really understand. I had to keep child-proof locks on absolutely everything. He could open any kind of door, even when he was really young. He could climb up to the top of the refrigerator too. But he could also be very destructive. As I said, he has no filter. When he was three, he would do things like break a window and jump out, or I'd have him in the car and he'd have a temper tantrum and he would roll the window down and throw out his glasses. We went through so many pairs of glasses. Psychiatrists told us he had a lot of anger. He went for one psychological exam when he was four – he was a bit young for that but the psychiatrist wanted to do it, and in the exam, he did things like throw the stuffed animals around and try to 'bite' the doctor with a plastic dinosaur. It was shortly after that that I realized that he had problems far beyond the typical problems children with special needs have."

"How did you realize this?"

"I went into his room where he had all these toy trains. He had a picnic basket and he was having a picnic with those trains, with inanimate objects. Most kids will bond with a doll or stuffed animal, but with him, it was always inanimate objects. Everything he drew was black. I remember the first time he drew a picture in color…he was about six years old. I also remember the first time he hugged me. He was also about six then. He had a speech delay so he couldn't talk until long after his peers. But he would do things, really self-destructive things. For instance, he got upset with me because I was talking to someone at a party. They had a high porch, about four or feet high, and he just dove off right onto the concrete. After I picked him up and calmed him down, he did it again."

"At this time, did you know for sure there was something wrong? Or did you just suspect it?"

"Oh, no, we definitely knew something was wrong and that it wasn't a matter of simple bad behavior. He had some medical issues when he was born and we had a genetics test done. About six weeks later we learned he had the extra chromosome. So we knew very early that something was wrong, but we didn't really know what that meant. We didn't know what to expect. As a rule, Klinefelter babies are easy to deal with. They don't cry a lot. Charles was like that. You could tell he was smart. He had high intelligence, but he just did strange things. When he was little, I took him to a Klinefelter specialist in Washington DC and she told us to put him in a Montessori school until we could get him into the regular special needs preschool. He was about two when I got him into that. At the same time, we were putting him in a lot of therapy, OT, PT, and Speech. We gave him early childhood intervention where the therapists came to our house. The one that really made a difference was the head of the Ph.D. department for speech disorders here at the local medical school. She saw Charles twice a week for a year and never charged us. I think he was such an extreme case that they wanted to work with him. One of the therapists was named Laura and the first words he ever said were 'Call Doctor Laura.'"

"Did he go to special needs schools?"

"Yes. Very early on we got him into a special needs preschool. He went there until he was six years old and we switched him to a special school for kids who have learning disabilities, dyslexia, dysgraphia and that sort of thing. A lot of those kids go on to college, so when Charles got accepted there we were really excited. I went on the board of the school. We still had a lot of hope for him back when he was really young. In those years, there were a lot of other kids who were doing the sort of things Charles was doing, but even then, there were problems with stigma and socialization. I would invite some of the kids over to ride his pony. Most of those kids had special needs, but even so, most of them only came once and never came back again. Even some of my family members or friends would come out once but would never come back again."

"But you still had hope in those early years?"

"You're always hoping. You have these bright spots. Sometimes things would be going great. We would get all these great academic reports. In fourth grade, we got some reports that showed he was at a high school senior level. Typical Asperger's Syndrome kid. When he was in seventh grade, it was at a college level. At ninth grade, he was at a post-doctoral level. So he's smart – he's *very* smart – but he has absolutely no common sense. We had him in social therapy for years, but it didn't work. He did things no other kid in his class would do. I think the only reason his school put up with it for as long as they did was because I was on the board. As he and his classmates in that school got older, they matured and he did not. He was getting great academic reports but he did not progress socially. He ended up having to leave that school because he had so many social problems. It was so awful, and so sad. He once paid a kid a hundred dollars just to play with him. It was money he took out of his piggy bank."

"Did he ever talk to you about being upset about these things?" I asked.

"No. Now that he's older and he's been in therapy so long and matured a lot, he's better about that. Honestly, I don't think he remembers a lot about those early years. If he does, maybe he wants to forget it. Think about it: as far as stigma goes, it's pretty bad when you're in a special needs school where every kid has LD and you *still* have stigma. At the end of his time there, one of the little girls in his class had a birthday party. A van came to pick up all the kids in the class. Every single child in that class got picked up except for Charles. He was the only one not invited. He went to get in the van and they pushed him out on the ground. In spite of all that, I was really upset when he was kicked out of that first special school."

"Where did he go after that?"

"He went to another that was sort of the last-chance school. It was very small. Most of the kids there have Aspergers, though many have other things too. A lot of them are really smart too, so Charles got along fairly well there at first. The teachers were excellent. It was a better program for him. Of course, the minute I saw the other kids and how disabled they were, my first thought was that Charles didn't belong there, and that he was only there because he got kicked out of the other school. That's what I told myself. But then he did some things. He put viruses on the school computers and knocked them all out. He was having a lot of social problems too. When he turned fifteen, his psychiatrist and psychologist recommended we send him to a boarding school up in Utah that was something like a psychiatric facility. We did as they suggested and sent him to that school. They assured us they could help him, and after a lot of time and a great deal of money, they told us no, they couldn't help him."

"What happened then?" I asked.

"He went to a second boarding school where there were only eight kids and their therapist was within ten feet of them all the time. The good thing about that place was they could really focus on him. When he acted inappropriately, they could help him understand what he was doing wrong. But this is what he's like: one day he just decided he wasn't going to do anything. He sat in a chair in mega-time out. He couldn't talk to anyone. He couldn't join in any activity or eat with the others. And he did that for three months! He refused to move. So that's the sort of thing I've been dealing with."

"It sounds like Charles, you, and your husband faced a great deal of stigma right from the beginning," I said.

"We did. It was so difficult. Even when he was really young, he had serious social troubles. When Halloween came around, there would be no children to go trick-or-treating with him. My husband and I took him around, and the whole time we passed small groups of kids dressed up in costume, and there was Charles, alone with his parents. When he was a little older, his social problems just got worse. He didn't know how to function in the world. I remember he wanted to play soccer. He was so excited about it that he slept in his soccer gear the night before the first game, but once he went out onto the field, he would just sit down and dig holes rather than playing. It was heartbreaking to watch."

"And you began to avoid these situations?"

"Yes. We moved several times. We did that for a lot of reasons, but avoiding neighbors was a big one for me. Any tight-knit neighborhood meant that everyone knew about Charles's problems. When he went to the treatment center in Utah, that was even worse. Some of the kids went there because they had bi-polar disorder or drug addictions. We were very depressed about having him go there. I remember going to a friend's house and one of her acquaintances, a woman, came over to visit. I went to the bathroom and when I came back I could tell that my friend had told this woman about Charles. I could tell. I had another friend who invited us over. There were some girls there and they were in the pool with Charles. He said something to them, I don't remember what it was, and suddenly everyone started whispering about him. The girls avoided him. Everyone avoided him. He went for years without a playdate of any kind."

"Was he ever on medication?"

"Yes, he was. The first year he was with the psychiatrist at age three, we didn't put him on any medication because they wanted to find out if his problems were a result of other things, such as a parenting problem or a psychological issue that medication wouldn't help. Eventually, they discovered they had to put him on medication. But now that he lives at my parents…"

"How is that working out?"

"Great. He loves it there and they love having him. We had to send him there because we had moved into an apartment in the same building where we have our office. When Charles came home from the treatment center in Utah, we discovered he was sneaking out at night and hanging out with homeless people under a bridge and even going to strip joints. He would sneak out and go there. We had no idea this was going on! We were having trouble waking him up in the morning and had no idea he had been out all night."

"How old was he?"

"Seventeen. That's when he came back to the school in the industrial park. Eventually the other kids at the school didn't want anything more to do with him, and the parents all wanted him gone. So after all these schools and facilities, we had to face the fact that none of them would work so we sent him out to live at my parent's place. He doesn't have to do anything there and it suits him fine. He's been there for a year and a half. He has gained a lot of weight because he doesn't do anything, but we feel we don't have any more options. A group home will never work for him because he'll run away. I don't know what we're going to do. My parents are in their seventies and I don't know how much longer they're going to be able to keep him there. We really don't know what's going to happen. We're probably going to have to hire someone to live with him. Here's another thing: we took him with us everywhere. When Charles hit middle school, my husband and I were rarely able to go out alone because we couldn't find a babysitter who would deal with him. We finally did get a mentor for him. It was incredible. We had gone through baby-sitting services but didn't have any luck. Finally we found a guy in college who had heard about Charles and wanted to try to help. He didn't even want to charge us. Obviously we paid him, but he's still Charles's only friend."

"It sounds to me as if difficulties with social skills are at the heart of Charles's troubles. They have taken over his life."

"They have. They have affected everything. I remember one time when we were at a neighborhood place and sitting in the parking lot, and a group of boys and girls walked by. Charles asked me if they were on a group date. It was just so sad. Now that he's older, his social skills are better. Those therapy places made a huge difference as far as social skills go. Another thing that was a blessing was when we finally realized that Charles is who he is, and that he is that way because of his disabilities. It is not because of something we did, or society did. You can't change a chromosome. Looking back at it now, I see that some of the difficulties were all about me. I'm pretty competitive and some of my friends have kids who are doing all these incredible things, learning Chinese, and doing really well in school. I compared myself to them. When he went to the school for kids with LD, I became super-LD-Mom,"

"Do your friends ever ask you where Charles is? Or do they just not want to talk about it?"

"Acquaintances and people I don't know very well will ask about him, but friends often do not."

"And family?"

"I've recently noticed that my parents are finally starting to admit there's something wrong with him. They refused to believe it before."

"Have you lost friendships over it?"

"I have. Some of those friendships were superficial. You understand that pretty quickly. I began to notice we were never invited to anything. No birthday parties, no summer picnics. I used to get really upset with my in-laws. There were two different families of in-laws. One had a child who was Charles' age. They only invited him over one time when he was about five and they never invited him back. The other family was very sweet to him. They would invite him over and were very understanding. For years I was really upset with the first family for completely ignoring him."

I told Serena her story was more intense and posed many more challenges than most others I've heard. "Surely you have learned some lessons along the way," I said. "They came painfully, but I have a feeling there may be others in your situation who are hoping to avoid some of the problems you faced."

"Here is what I would tell them," Serena said (and here I lay out her advice as bullet-points of hard-won wisdom).

• Do absolutely everything you can to the best of your abilities and resources so that you will be able to look at yourself in a mirror in twenty years and know for a fact that nothing more could have been done. You want to do this because the problem ain't going away. One very difficult issue is that everything involved with disabilities is so expensive. It was very expensive to treat a kid like Charles. You end up spending thousands on therapies from the time they're little. Many people don't have the resources to do that, but it's important to do the very best you can.

• Realize that most people will have absolutely no way of identifying with the troubles you are experiencing. They won't understand why your kid can't do the "normal" things that others can – especially when your child looks normal and doesn't have a "special needs" look.

• Some people are going to blame you for your child's problems and that is just how it is going to be. You have to constantly work to forgive them because otherwise, you will drive yourself crazy with anger and frustration.

• Face it. You are going to get embarrassed and that's all there is to it.

• Be a little circumspect. I sometimes wish I hadn't been so open about some of Charles' problems because I routinely "vented" and gave people too much information. No one needs to know that your toddler broke windows a few times and jumped out or was running around in the yard at night in the middle of the winter wearing only a diaper.

• For me, hope was a double-edged sword. Hope helped us through the first thirteen years because we thought if we worked hard with him or got him all the right therapies, he would be able to attend a good school, go to college, get a job and get married. It gave us strength, but unfortunately, false hope made it more difficult to discern what was a genuine possibility and what was fantasy.

• How much I have changed! I'm now so proud that he will soon be trying out new jobs through a program set up by a non-profit that works with businesses to find jobs for people like Charles. He may end up working scooping ice cream or bussing tables, but that's fine. I'm very proud that he graduated from high school-and, as odd as it sounds, I'm even more proud and grateful that he has never been in jail. How our priorities change! I went from having everything be all about me and my ego to having everything be all about Charles and his desires.

• There is an old saying that God never gives you more than you can handle. In my case, at least, I think that God gave me what I needed. I changed from a hyper-competitive parent to one who understands and recognizes that success comes in many different forms. Loving my son for who he is and not what I want him to be has been an incredible gift.

• Finally, I would like you to remember this. Hope may waver but love endures. Love your child. Love him the way he is and not who you want him to be. Love him. Love him. Forgive him. Love him more – and love yourself.

SOMETHING SOCIETY WANTED ME TO BE ASHAMED OF

Natalie

My quest to speak with a young adult with LD who had experienced stigma next led me to Natalie Tamburello, the program associate for learning resources & research at the National Center for Learning Disabilities (NCLD). Natalie not only has LD herself but is making a difference in the lives of others with LD through her work as a professional, an activist, and a volunteer. Prior to joining the NCLD team, Natalie served as the program director for Student Advisors for Education (SAFE), the student branch of the Parents Education Network (PEN). After leaving SAFE, she developed an empowerment program for incarcerated adults with learning disabilities.

After graduating Magna Cum Laude with a BA in Psychology from Whitman College in Walla Walla, Washington, she completed a M.Phil in Education at the University of Cambridge in England, focusing on leadership within the LD/ADHD community and the emerging learning rights movement. Her many volunteer activities focus on non-profit organizations serving students underrepresented in our education system. With all her successes, you wouldn't think stigma has touched her life, but it has.

This is her story:

I grew up in San Francisco and attended a K -12 French immersion school, where students receive a dual diploma including the International Baccalaureate. All the classes are in French, with the sole exception of English class. Almost immediately after starting first grade, there was an obvious issue with my reading and my ability to spell and write. I could speak French and English fluently but I could neither spell nor read. I was able to learn to speak and understand French because language acquisition at an early age is far easier than later in life.

My parents told me that I started acting out in first grade as reading, writing and spelling were introduced. I begged to stay home, complaining of stomach aches. Like so many kids with LD, I'd find any excuse not to read. I would get up when it was my turn to read, I was unable to sit in my seat, I would also go to the bathroom – anything to avoid the reading problem. And at some point, I resisted reading aloud altogether, electing to get out of my seat and sing along instead. Professionals at the school were called in to observe me in my classes and told my parents I was a "behavioral problem." My parents refused to accept this and they investigated further. I was screened at the school and at the end of first grade I was referred to a specialist who documented my dyslexia, which was described to my parents this way: 'Natalie knows what is going on, but she is extremely frustrated because she can't communicate how smart she is with the world.'

Some teachers believed this was due learning two languages, but everyone else was taking the same curriculum and succeeding, while I wasn't. And it wasn't only French; I wasn't spelling or reading English either. I wasn't reading at all. My friends were reading chapter books in the first and second grades while I was still attempting phonics. By second grade, I was so embarrassed by what I was reading that my mom would buy book covers so no one would know that I was reading simple phonics books with no word in the book series more than three letters long. Even at age seven, I knew that my difference was something society wanted me to be ashamed of. I didn't want anyone to know what was going on. I felt the effects of stigma immediately.

I didn't have many friends at that school, though I really wanted to fit in. I remember all my classmates were obsessed with fantasy chapter books. They were all about dragons and mystical places and I really wanted to read them too, so my mom would buy them for me and she read them to me so I could talk about them with friends. But I knew I wasn't *reading* them. I knew I wasn't capable of reading them. My mom tells this story where one day she found me in my bedroom, sobbing and all my books were all over the floor. I was just so frustrated because it seemed I was always surrounded by books at home and at school and I couldn't read any of them. I would pick up, try to read it, realize I couldn't do it, and throw it on the floor. Pick up another, try again, and throw it on the floor. I knew it was possible to get a story from them but I didn't know *how* to do it. Everybody else seemed to get it and I didn't. I felt like I didn't belong.

I think I did a really good job of hiding it and compensating. I didn't realize it at the time, but I was discovering other strengths. I acted like I'd read the chapter books, for I was a good listener and retained what I heard. The rest, I made up. I also knew that learning through kinesthesia worked well for me. (Note: Kinesthetic learning is when learning takes place by students carrying out physical activities, rather than listening to a lecture or watching demonstrations.) I remember asking to go up to the board in front of the class to work on a problem – and of course, I only did this when it was something I felt confident about. At that age I was good at math so I didn't hesitate to volunteer to go to the board to work out a math problem whenever possible. I was hoping that if I overcompensated by showcasing my strengths, no one would notice my weaknesses. My mom observed this kinesthetic strength at home because we had a big white board and I'd shown a clear preference for it. When my mom encouraged my teacher to let me use the board more regularly, the teacher had already concluded I was a behavior problem and said: "I think it's about Natalie wanting to bring attention to herself and I can't have her going to the board all the time. She needs to learn like the others."

I desperately wanted to show that I was intelligent and had even discovered accommodations that served me well, but I was not only precluded from using them, any effort to do things differently was seen as disruptive and unacceptable. I was stigmatized., but I was desperate to show that I wasn't "dumb" and wanted to show some skills in ways that seemed to work for me. I hoped to distract from those things I knew I couldn't do. I tried to take every opportunity possible to succeed. Sometimes it didn't work. When I was called on to something I knew I couldn't do, I became the class clown and that provided me with some cover. Students laughed because I was funny, not because I was failing in front of them.

It was so challenging to be so different from my classmates. I remember we had these little name placards and we had to learn to write our name in cursive and I just dreaded writing out my name. My last name is Tamburello, which I thought was unbelievably long. The "bur" part of my name always confused me. It was all memorization and I was constantly doubting if I did anything right, even when I had.

Self-doubt, especially when it comes to spelling and writing continues to be a challenge to this day. For example, I still wonder if I've written an email or report well enough and wonder how much is misspelled, before turning it in or pushing "Send." If I get edits back, I feel like I've messed up and I have to be reassured that everyone's work gets edited and everyone makes mistakes. For me it's so ingrained that I am always nervous, much more so than everyone else.

Things became worse in second grade, much worse, and my reading, even with outside support was not improving. I didn't want to go to school. I hated my teachers and all of education felt tortuous. At the end of second grade my parents received a letter from the school, advising that I would not be permitted to return the following year. I had been kicked out.

My parents struggled greatly with the label issue after that first diagnosis. They continued to face more challenging decisions as the nature of my cognitive differences began to unfold. They were unsure about sending me to a special school for fear it would permanently mark me as different and separate. They were terrified for my future in a world that didn't seem to recognize the value in people like me. They were consumed with doubts and worries. Do we put her in a school that's more accommodating? Do we keep her where she is with additional help?

I think there were two things during this time that helped my parents significantly. One is that my mother has a brother who definitely has learning issues and she saw how he struggled in school. This was her youngest brother, and her busy parents assigned her to do homework with him every night. She saw how he struggled and, back then, little was understood about how he learned. I think she didn't want that to happen to me. Second, my parents did a really good job surrounding themselves with people who knew what to do. They reached out to friends and professionals to help and advise them. If they didn't know what to do, they would find someone who did.

I think my father might have had more uncertainty and fear for my future than my mother. If my mother did, she never showed it. I don't think my father ever fully understood what was going on. He was frustrated that school was hard for me, that so much was uncertain, that my mom was constantly working with me, and that everything took so much effort. In short, family life was not what he expected and he didn't know what to do about it. My mother seemed better able to understand and cope with me because she had seen it before and she was helping me with homework every day so she sort of "got" how I learned and she often made it fun. For example when it was time to learn words, she'd make a game of it: I didn't say the word aloud: I acted it out. For example, if the word spelled "r-u-n", I ran. It was fun and it was kinesthetic, and I'd remember running when I saw the word "run" which helped me remember the word. That's the thing about dyslexia: nothing about reading becomes automatic. Every word is a struggle to decode and commit to memory. Frankly, it's exhausting.

Both of my parents are attorneys. They had planned to be full-time attorneys and the reality of my diagnosis meant my mother worked part-time and moved her office to our home. She realized she needed to spend more time with me – for both of us. That was a big compromise for them. I'm sure she had some qualms with that and was very frustrated. She was forty when I was born, and was well established in her career, so it was a big change.

After I was told I could no longer attend the French immersion school, my parents tried to transition me into other schools that were more accommodating but with the academic record I had, either I wasn't sufficiently acceptable, or there was no space available. I eventually attended the Charles Armstrong School, which is a special ed school in Belmont, California, specifically for children with specific learning disabilities. My parents struggled with this decision. They visited the school separately and each had the identical experience: when the tour was completed, they returned to the car and cried. They were so uncertain about what was best for me. The school, as my mom described it, "was anything but mainstream. If our daughter doesn't belong here, this will be a terrible decision. If, on the other hand, this is where she'll learn best, then shame on us for not sending her here." I started there in third grade and stayed through fifth grade. My parents said it was the best decision they ever made.

After a few years at Charles Armstrong, I transitioned back to a mainstream school. That was also a difficult time because I had been successful at Armstrong and once again I was faced with that familiar fear of being different. I ended up at a very small middle school with eighteen kids in my class and, frankly, it was awful. Academically awful. Socially awful. I was completely ostracized by all the girls. I still don't know why. I guess it just happens with girls in middle school, especially when one is an outsider joining a small group of girls who have been friends since kindergarten. There seemed to be competition even when there really wasn't competition. There was one girl in particular who just despised me. She was the ringleader in the class and was determined to exclude me and make sure the other girls did as well. I am still clueless about the source of her cruelty toward me. She just needed to be the best and the most popular and, perhaps as an outsider, I was somehow threatening. I worked really hard at my academics and sometimes received grades that were better than hers and this seemed intolerable to her.

Most of the teachers were wonderfully accommodating, but there was one teacher who did not like the fact that my mother and my learning specialist helped me with homework. She thought I was cheating because they edited my work. She saw the way I spelled in class and saw the difference in my homework, but neither my mother nor the specialist ever did my homework for me. My process was this: if I had a paper for homework I would dictate it to my mom. She was adamant about not doing the work for me. If she helped with editing something, she offered comments about whether something was confusing, and spelling errors were in track changes on the computer so I could *see* all the changes. It was very laborious but it taught me a lot about how to "see" my writing and advocate for myself. Even so, the teacher thought I was cheating and reprimanded me as well as my mom. Luckily, our learning specialist advocated for us both and assured the teacher there was no cheating going on, but it undermined my self-confidence greatly.

I eventually found a friend, another transfer student, who came the year after I entered. We became real friends, the only one I had, and that was all I needed. Years later, I realized that all the kids I befriended throughout my school years were different in some way. They all had learning disabilities or were students of color – outsiders to the mainstream, like me. Something in their life had caused them to feel alienated or different. There was a kinship based on that shared experience, even though I didn't really understand that at the time. I guess because I saw that they too felt alone in certain situations, I could empathize – especially during middle school. I think when kids experience feeling different and not fitting in, they find each other.

If I were to meet a young person who is really struggling with being bullied or with feelings of inadequacy, I would offer a few words of advice. I would share some of my experiences and tell them that the most important thing for me was making sure I had a community and making sure I had a place where I felt like I was smart and that I belonged. I would ask them to tell me what their favorite thing is, to describe what they love, or what they feel passionate about. For me it was singing. I would make sure that is a priority in their life because the confidence that came from an extracurricular activity can translate into school confidence. Kids can find friends who value them for who they are. It helps to try to find a friend or two, or better yet, a community. It was transformational for me to go to a special school and get to know other kids like me. It helped me realize that it wasn't just me. I knew I wasn't alone. The code of silence was not needed. I knew it wasn't my fault. And importantly, the teachers there knew how to teach me in a way that made sense to me.

My mother also had a habit of asking what would make things better when I wasn't able or willing to do things like homework.

I remember telling her once, "If we built a fort and read in there, that might make it better." It gave me the time to mentally prepare to do something I didn't really want to do and it made it a little more fun than it otherwise would be. I had control over that one aspect of reading, so even though it didn't help me know how to read, it put me in a better mindset. That concept opened up a lot of doors for my parents. They learned to approach things differently, and that, in turn, helped empower me to discover how I learn best. When they saw me challenged, they would consider asking me my opinions on what would make things easier for me. They then made sure that everything that worked for me actually happened. I think so many parents threaten to take activities away, often the very activities in which their child excels and loves best, when kids don't do well academically. I think that's a huge mistake. The kids then have nothing they love or excel in. It's awful.

I would also say parents should put family relationships over academics. For instance, there would be many times in middle school when I would get in the car and I would just start sobbing. I had held in all these horrible experiences and feelings from the school day and I just let go as soon as I got into the car. My mother, instead of worrying about all the homework I had to do that night, would drop all plans, and we would go to a little crepe shop to talk about the day. We would debrief over our crepes and come away with a game plan for the next day. She really valued our relationship and being open and honest. She also understood that a productive hour was wisely spent helping me figure out what I could do to make things better tomorrow. She didn't tell me what to do or coddle me, but she included me, listened to me, and guided me through my plans. That was huge. I was very lucky.

Having LD taught me how to work harder, how to manage my time, and how to work around things. So many things were so difficult for so long that I learned to deal with challenges. Most kids without LD don't experience that. I had to learn *how* I learn at a very young age and it served me well. I distinctly remember being in an advanced chemistry class in college. I was struggling and it was hard, and there were things I didn't understand, but I had already learned that if something wasn't working, I would try something else until I found the path that did work. The other kids were saying things like, 'I got a C, so I'm dropping out.' They were essentially saying, 'If I don't get it, if I don't succeed, I'm done'. It wasn't, 'If I don't get it, what can I do to get it?' They hit a wall and that was it. So for me, I would have to say that even though the struggles of having LD were very painful, I certainly learned a lot from them and I rarely back down from a challenge.

"SHOULD I GET YOU A SOBBING TOWEL?

"Steve"

A S mentioned several times in this book, I have had a difficult time finding a young adult with truly severe LD who would talk to me about stigma. Just when I began to despair of ever finding such a person, I received a call from a friend who told me her son had agreed to open up about his life. I had already tried several times without success to speak with him, but he finally agreed to speak into a dictation machine with no one around.

I was specific in my request to tell his story, and also to offer some suggestions on how best to handle the stigma that life can sometimes throw our way. He did the first, but was unable to do much with the second.

Some of us our wounded by stigma to such an extent that we can be rendered speechless by any attempt to find a silver lining. I believe "Steve" is one of those people. His is a painful story to read, and though I wish I could tell you things have improved since he told his story one night, all alone, into a dictation machine, I have reason to believe things have pretty much remained the same for him.

Here then is "Steve", telling us how stigma came into his life and chose to stay.

When Anne Ford told my mother she was having trouble finding someone with severe learning disabilities who would talk openly about their experiences with stigma, my mother suggested I might be willing to talk to her. When my mother told me this, my first reaction was a shouted "NO!" and I refused to talk about it any more. She came back to the subject a few months later and told me I didn't have to give my real name or where I lived or where I worked, and so I agreed. But when the day came to meet with Mrs. Ford, I called with an excuse. I told her I was sick. It was just like when I was back in school and I didn't want to face something. When she rescheduled, I called with another excuse.

Finally, Mrs. Ford suggested we not meet in person and if I spoke into a tape recorder that would be a way to tell my story. It's better for me too because I'm a terrible writer. I sometimes have thoughts that sound really good but when I try to put them on paper or type them, it doesn't come out the way I want. For example, if I wanted to say "the sky was blue, with high fluffy white clouds and the air was crisp and clear," it comes out as "It was a nice day" when I write it.

So I am talking into a tape recorder. I might ramble sometimes, so I apologize.

I changed my real name to "Steve". I am twenty-eight years old. I have an older sister who is a financial advisor. My younger brother is in his second year of law school. I work in maintenance and run the freight elevator at a large building in my town.

My mother has told me over and over that I am intelligent. She has read articles to me with experts saying that people with my kind of LD have average to above-average intelligence. So I know that on one level, but I have been called stupid and retarded so many times in my life that I can't help but feel that about myself sometimes. Even a teacher one time asked me if I was retarded. I never told my parents about that. I was too ashamed.

I was diagnosed with severe LD when I was in fourth grade. Dyslexia, dysgraphia, dyscalculia, you name it, I have it. I have every "dys" there is. I also have trouble with social issues. And of course, I can't read very well and my writing is awful. But above all, having trouble with all the "dys" is nothing compared to the social troubles I have had because of my LD.

Before fourth grade, everybody just thought I was stupid. Even my grandfather used to tell people I was a little slow. I can remember him telling one of his friends that. "Steve is a little slow". I didn't know what it meant at the time. I thought he meant I walked slow. My mother suspected something was wrong. If it wasn't for her, I don't know what would have happened to me. She kept insisting that the school I was going to evaluate me. Finally I was tested and found to have LD.

I just called my mother to ask what the school said I had. She told me they said I had multiple, severe learning disabilities.

So I was diagnosed in fourth grade, but by then I had already heard so many times that I was dumb and lazy and not trying hard enough that I believed it. It's just awful when you are trying as hard as you can, and trying ten times more than everyone else in the class, only to hear the teacher say you would do better if only you weren't so lazy. It didn't matter how many times I told her I was trying and I was doing the work. She didn't believe it. I can remember one time…you know what? It's so awful, it still makes me get tense.

In third grade, Mrs. V told me I wasn't trying and I was lazy, and I was so frustrated, I got tears in my eyes. In front of the whole class, she said, "Should I go get you a sobbing towel?" I didn't know what a sobbing towel was. I *still* don't know. But it was so embarrassing. Everyone in the class started laughing and I had everything I could do not to cry more. It was just awful. And I can remember that experience like it happened yesterday. As I remember it, that's when stigma started. From that day on, I was stigmatized by my classmates and my teachers. My life took a total change.

Even after being diagnosed I was still called names. I was put in special education, and I don't care what anyone says. The fact that you are put in special ed singles you out. I don't know why they can't figure out a way to make it easier. Our special ed classes were at the end of a hall where there were no other classrooms. Whenever anyone went down that hall, it was obvious where they were going. There was one kid in my class named Edward who also had LD and some of the older kids used to call him "Special Ed".

It was embarrassing and it was awkward. It was humiliating to go down that hall. It caused me problems with social skills. I think I could have talked to people easy enough, but I was so beaten down by the thought that I was stupid that I couldn't get the courage to talk to anyone. I would see a group of kids in the hall and I wanted to talk to them. I wanted to be in that group and be friends with them, but when I got closer, I felt like they didn't want to talk to me, or what if they started talking about things I didn't understand, or what if they said I was one of those special ed "retards"?   And so I didn't say anything. I walked by them looking at the floor.

I think it broke my mother's heart to know I didn't have any friends all through school, but it wasn't her fault. I just couldn't seem to click with anyone.

Eventually I did find some friends but they weren't the right kinds of friends. I know that now. I am determined to be honest when talking about my story, so I need to tell this part too. I got into what my father called "the wrong crowd". I started smoking marijuana when I was sixteen and it was the first time I felt like I fit in. There were a few others in our school who were stoners and they didn't care if I had LD or not. But I got in some trouble with that, so I had to give up that life.

I dropped out of high school in my senior year. I didn't see the point of going on. I see the point now, but I didn't back then. Back then, I thought "why should I put up with this?   It is like going to be tortured every day." There were a couple of teachers who really tried to help me, but it was no use. No matter what they did, I couldn't really improve. Most of the other teachers long ago gave up on me. I think they just passed me on to the next grade to get rid of me.

That's really kind of how I felt most of my life, that people were just trying to get rid of me. I hope I don't sound like I'm full of self-pity. I don't mean to sound that way. I don't really feel sorry for myself either. That's just the way it is. When I say people try to get rid of me, I mean they put up with me only as long as they have to and then they go away. Like in a conversation, I have trouble following what people are saying so I either say the wrong thing or make a comment long after the conversation has moved on to another subject. I also don't really do well with humor. Sometimes I say something I think is funny and, instead, people get offended or they look at me like I am insane.

You see why I spend so much time by myself? It's easier that way.

I have a job in maintenance. If I think about my brother and sister and their success, I get a little bothered. At the same time, I am happy to have this job. I am sure if I didn't have LD, I would have gone to college and maybe even veterinarian school. That was always my dream to be a vet, but that will never happen. I am thinking about getting my GED so I will have my high school degree, but even now, when I think about going to classes, I get a pit in my stomach. I really do. All the old feelings come back and I think well, maybe not. Maybe things are fine like they are.

So that's it. I'm sorry if my story seemed too much of a downer. I tried to be honest.

Mrs. Ford asked if I had any advice. I guess what I would tell parents is to be as much like my mother as possible. She is the one person who always stood by me and accepted me and tried to help me. She still does (who do you think is pushing for the GED diploma?). I don't think I always show it, but I really, really appreciate it. I don't know what my life would be like without her. Much worse, that's for sure.

And if you have LD, try to stay positive. You know what? Those people who say things and call you names are ignorant. They really are. I hope you will do what I did not do, and try to find at least one friend who understands you and accepts you for who you are.

STIGMA

A Professional View

ANOTHEIR KIND OF NORMAL

Questions and Answers with Dr. Sheldon Horowitz

When I served as Chair of the National Center for Learning Disabilities, I was lucky enough to work with Dr. Sheldon Horowitz, one of the top experts in the field of learning disabilities and one of the most compassionate professionals I have had the pleasure to meet. Dr. Horowitz has guided and comforted thousands of parents over the years, and has done so with rare patience, understanding and good humor. I could think of no better person to turn to for advice and insight into the painful experiences associated with stigma.

Stigma is Always Negative

QUESTION: How would you suggest we think about the word stigma?

DR. HOROWITZ: Stigma is the silent killer of success and no one should underestimate its power. It can undo well-deserved feelings of accomplishment, undermine a hard-earned sense of pride, and diminish the self-worth that we know is a critical driver of success in life for every person, not just those with learning and attention issues.

It can be triggered by reality or fantasy and is difficult or even impossible to measure, but it is very real, often unpredicted, and always negative. Once stigma enters a person's life, it is not easily undone and almost never forgotten. Living with stigma is extraordinarily hard to do because the shadow it casts touches virtually every aspect of our lives.

Without offering a formal definition, I think it is fair to say that stigma can be described as a bundle of feelings that includes shame, fear, undeserved discredit, and disapproval. These feelings can result from how a person feels about themselves or about how they think others feel about them. Stigma can also result from judgments people make about conditions or characteristics they observe or ways they perceive differences in other's around them.

Is stigma really such a big deal? Try this quick exercise and the answer to the question will be clear. Read each of the short descriptions below about a stranger and ask yourself these questions: do I feel sorry for this person? Will this person be held back in some way from living a happy and productive life? Is this someone I could trust or even love?

- Joe was just released from prison
- Susan was born with a deformed spine and needs a wheelchair to get around
- Kelly is a former drug user who is HIV positive
- Debbie is battling depression

Now what if I told you that each of these people was a college graduate, had a well-paying job, and mentored kids after school? What just happened? Did your feeling change once you had new information? Well, that's how stigma works. It grabs hold of the negative associations, the pity and the discomfort that sneaks into our minds, and builds an invisible barrier that we don't often realize exists.

The roadblocks created by stigma are real and, unfortunately, can leave indelible impressions throughout a person's lifetime. The successful business owner who struggled with dyslexia as a child has vivid memories of being embarrassed in front of teachers and peers by mistakes while reading aloud in class or by failing grades on spelling tests. The young adult with ADHD who graduated college with honors whose exuberance during their early school years was misunderstood as careless disregard for rules or just plain bad behavior. Despite their successes, these individuals have vivid recollections of the burden of stigma imposed by others and the worry and doubt that result by being stigmatized by a label. And here's the rub: the very labels that are intended to protect a person from feelings of low self-esteem and provide them with services, supports and protections under law invite stigma to take hold and not let go.

So the first step to understanding and dealing with stigma is to recognize that it exists, understand that it happens both from within and outside each individual, and can have profound consequences for children, adolescents and adults, families, and society as a whole. When we combat stigma, we commit ourselves to valuing each person for who they are, their strengths and weaknesses, similarities and differences, and we celebrate all kinds of diversity, including that which results from having learning and attention issues.

It is safe to say that underlying stigma is a certain level of personal discomfort. Unless we're close to someone who lives with impaired hearing or vision, intellectual disabilities, a chronic medical condition, a mental health disorder, or issues like LD and ADHD, we are a little scared of it. Stigma associated with all these different kinds of things is a hard knot to untangle because it's not just about a person who happens to have a physical disorder or something different about them – it is also about people who look at them and make judgments about them. And then there is the problem of the person him or herself who is being judged and how they feel about being who they are.

Is it more complicated when a person's disabilities are "hidden?"

I wouldn't say it's more complicated, but it certainly more subtle. Learning disabilities are often hidden until a person is required to perform tasks that tap their particular areas of weakness. When meeting someone with LD or ADHD for the first time, it would not be uncommon to assume that they are fast and efficient readers, skilled at math computation and problem solving, good at spelling and written expression, and well organized, able to plan, initiate and complete tasks without difficulty. And then it happens: they are asked to do simple math, follow a series of directions, or take written notes. Up until that point, LD or ADHD are invisible. Not only is it a surprise for the person who is looking in from the outside, but it's a reality check for the person with LD or ADHD who now wonders how it will affect their relationship with them and whether others will shape impressions about them based on stigma stereotypes. Unfortunately, once formed, stigma is hard to undo, both for the person who struggles and for outsiders whose assumptions were the result of misinformation or hastily formed conclusions.

We talk a lot about the levels or types of stigma. One type we have been calling "self-stigma". We think of this when people reflect how they have been treated by society. Over time, they begin to view themselves as having a reason to be stigmatized. We heard of a young man who attended an orientation program at a school for teenagers with LD. He was a tall, blond, surfer-type and he took one look at the other kids and said, "Oh no, no, I can't go to this school." He felt a sense of stigma toward them but also toward himself. He knew nothing about the students at this school. His reaction was solely based on his fear of being stigmatized by the LD label and by association with students who were already associated with the label. Is this common?

There are so many different ways that LD manifests itself, so it stands to reason that people with LD will react in different ways to having LD. Some will be open and will readily disclose their LD to others. Some will try to hide their LD, even if it denies them access to services and supports.

One of the most complicated aspects of having LD for some individuals has to do with the social domain. Learning disabilities and related disorders such as ADHD are most often associated with problems in academic skills and areas such as short-term or working memory, but they can also have a significant impact on social skills. This surfer-type adolescent may have reacted unfavorably to being associated with other kids with LD who are less socially savvy, who miss social cues, or who have a hard time with word play or humor; all of which make them stand out in ways that seem immature or just not cool. The most telling part of this story, however, is that he didn't even give them a chance. He judged without knowledge. He let stigma win without putting up a fight.

Do you believe stigma can be overcome or, at least, avoided?

The better a person with LD knows about their needs as a learner, the more comfortable they will feel living with their LD. Self-awareness leads to the ability to share the reality of their world with others, which, in turn, allows them to trouble-shoot the environment and set up certain protective strategies or coping strategies that help them stay positive about their ability to succeed. It also leads to a level of comfort and confidence that will be noticed by others. I can't stress enough how important it is for parents to help children develop the social skills they need to become effective self-advocates before they transition out of high school. Sure, having nurturing and protective parents is essential during the early years, but it's a mistake to assume that kids will know what to do just because they reach adolescence or young adulthood. One of the most troubling statistics in the State of Learning Disabilities Report conducted by The National Center for Learning Disabilities (NCLD) is that while 95% of students with LD receive accommodations in high school, only 17% request them after they graduate and enter college and the workforce. That is another unfortunate win for stigma

Is it possible that stigma about LD is fueled by a lack of public awareness about the condition?

That is certainly part of the problem. NCLD conducted a national online survey, asking a random sample of 2000 adults across the USA what they thought they know about LD. The results were astounding. 22% said that LD is caused by watching too much TV. 31% believed that poor diet can cause LD. 24% believed that LD could be caused by childhood vaccinations, a disproven argument associated with some parents of children with autism spectrum disorder. 43% believed that LD is associated with IQ, even though kids with LD, by definition, have to be of at least average intelligence. One third of the parents surveyed said a cause of LD was a lack of parent or teacher involvement during the early childhood years. 55% said that LD can be treated with corrective eyewear. Given this pervasive misunderstanding about LD, someone trying to get out from under the crosshairs of stigma is going to have a hard time.

The good news is that stigma does not have to win. When individuals with LD find their "voice" and get what they need to compete, the challenge then becomes how to deal with people who don't get it. For example, Dr. Carol Greier is a Nobel Laureate and professor of molecular biology at John's Hopkins School of Medicine who conducted breakthrough research in genetics. She has dyslexia.

Despite her obvious intellectual prowess, her journey through school was not easy. She recalls having to convince her teachers that she was a hard-working, highly motivated and capable student and that she was entitled to accommodations. When it came to applying to graduate school, she ended up not taking certain exams because she knew she wouldn't do well on them. She still ended up winning this prestigious award and becoming a faculty member at one of the most respected science institutions in the world.

It's really a shame that people with LD have to fight their way out of the shadow of stigma during their formative years. Too many never make it and end up burdened by feelings of inadequacy. They feel undervalued and underappreciated and they miss out on opportunities to explore their passions and follow their dreams.

I recall watching a TV show from the 1950s, where a man in a wheelchair entered a restaurant and everyone stopped talking and stared at him. The look on everyone's face was 'what is he doing here?' I remember being shocked both by the insensitivity of the diners and by the realization of how much society has changed since then. Today, no one would think twice about seeing a person in a wheelchair in a public place. In fact, they'd likely try to be helpful or accommodating. So this is the big question: how does society change from stigma into acceptance?

People are fearful of things they don't understand and change happens slowly. It takes time and practice for individuals with LD to discover their strengths and weaknesses and to talk about their disabilities without being embarrassed or fearful of isolation or rejection. The ability to tell a college professor or a manager at work 'this is what I need to succeed' or 'this is what I'm entitled to by law' just doesn't happen overnight. Asking a waiter to read a menu aloud is not something that comes easily. Requesting help from a colleague to proofread and edit emails or work documents takes courage, confidence and grit, but it should never be confused as a sign of weakness or reason for shame.

Society is certainly more accepting and welcoming of individuals with disabilities of all sorts, but we have a long way to go. Stigma can lurk silently and appear in ways that are unexpected, especially when it comes to learning and attention issues.

Is there a case for a special relationship between stigma and learning and attention issues?

Yes, there is, because of the size of the population. Again, if you look at the most recent data in NCLD's State of Learning Disabilities Report, you'll see that about 40% of all children who receive special education services in school are classified as having specific learning disabilities. Add this to the millions of children with ADHD, the many millions who reading and math scores on national assessments are "below proficient", and the millions more who require intensive instructional interventions to keep up with their peers, and you're talking about 1-in-5. Not all these students have documented disabilities, but their struggles are real and public education has made a commitment to catch them and help them succeed before they experience frustration and failure. Because of this changing culture in schools, the stigma associated with such things as getting extra help from a reading specialist or having access to read-aloud or note-taking technologies is becoming less pronounced. Perhaps it is overly optimistic, but in a way, having LD may be accepted more and more as "another kind of normal."

We haven't mentioned the impact of stigma on siblings and families. Almost everywhere we go we hear stories about parents not knowing how to talk to friends and family about their child who struggles with learning. We wrote an entire book about sibling issues called The Forgotten Child. In our research we heard parents speak, often with tears in their eyes, about feeling guilty that they didn't spend enough time with their kids who don't have LD. What about those siblings? Does stigma by association impact them?

Once more, the answer has to do with open and honest self-reflection and communication. Parents need to make choices all the time, and the closer they are to the nature of their child's struggle, the better able they are to provide just-in-time nurturing, support and guidance. Siblings without LD are just as deserving of attention and special time with parents, but there is no question that the frequency and intensity of attention will be different. When kids with LD are coming home every day feeling socially isolated, anxious, and overwhelmed by poor grades, projects looming and many hours of reading, writing and math due in short order, parents have no choice but to hyper-focus on the immediate school demands. Siblings will often hide feelings of resentment, not wanting to sound selfish or jealous, but wishing that the balance of attention in the family was tilted more toward center. Setting time for everyone to share what they are working on and even to complain out loud could help level the playing field in terms of expectations for parent attention.

The trick here (and it's never easy) is to find the right balance between the practical and emotional needs and desires of children and parents. And once you think you've got it figured out, it changes as a result of new circumstances, new demands, new opportunities and yes, even hormones! Home should be a safe haven for all, and that means making sure that everyone feels understood and appreciated, can ask for help, express frustrations and, hopefully, feel empowered to speak their mind and trouble-shoot solutions to problems, no matter how personal.

Parents love to talk about their kids, their grades, their achievements in sports, their musical prowess, you name it. This often gets complicated by LD. We've heard from parents that they dread having these conversations and tend to say nothing because they're afraid that the issue of LD will come up. What's a parent to do?

More than twenty years ago, I was sitting in my office with a family whose sixth grader had just undergone a comprehensive evaluation and was found to have a learning disability. After hearing the results of the testing, the parents got teary and worried out loud about the future. They even asked whether LD would hold her back from someday attending college. I turned to their child and asked her what she learned from the testing. With a big smile, she said 'I knew that I was smart, and now I have proof!' The next thing she said has stayed with me all these years. 'LD is what I have, but it's not who I am.' It was a three-Kleenex moment for sure, and one that made it possible for these parents to think of their daughter and her having LD in a very different way.

The truth is that LD is not something that a child leaves at the schoolhouse door. It is there in the supermarket, at the movies, on the soccer field, and at a sleepover. And while it poses obstacles to the ease with which someone masters and performs certain tasks, it does not diminish the wonder, enthusiasm and passion that each of us has inside. A child with dyscalculia could be fascinated by the challenges of math and science and pursue studies (and a career!) in medicine, astronomy, oceanography or physics. A child with dyslexia could become a poet, novelist, actor or journalist.

So back to the question: what is a parent to do? The answer is to think not about what their child struggles to *do* but rather who they *are*, how they embrace their challenges and persevere past obstacles to become comfortable in their own skin. It is fine for a parent to say that their child is not an "A" student or even that school is challenging, but it's not OK to be silent about the things they do well and that give them joy.

There are clearly times when stigma becomes a "family affair." Can you give some examples?

Stigma associated with LD can weigh heavily on families. It happens all the time, but some are more emotionally charged than others. Think about being in a house of worship and having a child who can't keep up or, in some instances, even participate in communal reading. Neighbors, friends or relatives seated nearby notice your child's struggle. You feel trapped, worried what they are thinking, fighting back feelings of shame, and wishing you could magically beam an explanation across the pews and assure them that your child's behavior is not a sign of disinterest or laziness.

You don't have to be out in public for these stigma-fraught moments to occur. Think about the Christmas dinner or gathering around the table at an Easter meal or a Passover Seder. Everyone is happy for great food and wonderful company, and it's time to go around the room, asking each person to read something aloud or to reflect aloud about things for which they are thankful. The child with learning and attention issues may not understand what they've been asked to do, and especially under pressure, may have difficulty selecting the right words to express their thoughts and struggle to express themselves in a way that captures their thoughts and feelings.

Anticipating the challenges of moments like these is not always possible, but planning and practice can go a long way. Parents might be tempted to jump in and speak for their child, but there's a much better approach. Have the child ask to skip their turn and then have the conversation circle back after others have spoken. Of course, if parents know that this type of sharing is likely to happen, they could take a few minutes ahead of time and help their child prepare what they would like to say. If there are "readings" that are done each year at these gatherings, getting them in advance and rehearsing with your child before the event could not only keep stigma at bay but help them (and you) feel proud and connected to friends and family at these important family times.

QUESTION: So it sounds like what it comes down to with Stigma is this: we accept that we can't change society and that we can't wave a magic wand that will make everyone more understanding. But we can do this: we can help create a child who can self-advocate and sail above the stigma. Does that state the case?

DR. HOROWITZ: I agree that there is no magic wand that will change the way people act and feel about learning disabilities, but I'm more than a little optimistic that society is changing in ways that could protect children and families from the harmful effects of stigma. Schools are becoming even more inclusive of children with all sorts of special needs and education law is focusing on how to strengthen teaching practices and ensure that schools are accountable for student learning. New technologies have made it easier for students with LD to get instruction that is personalized to their unique profiles and kids who struggle with learning are able to access demanding schoolwork through materials that are based on cutting-edge principles like Universal Design for Learning. All of these factors will make it easier to prevent and address stigma. Unfortunately, stigma is here to stay, but self-awareness, self-advocacy, open and honest communication, accurate information, focusing on strengths while addressing weaknesses, and a supportive community are all critical ways to counteract it.

I know someone who is blind and who filed a discrimination suit against a taxi driver (and won). The driver said that his Seeing Eye dog wasn't allowed into the cab. Could this ever apply to an LD situation?

If you're asking whether parents of children with LD sue school districts when they think their child is being denied a "free and appropriate education" the answer is yes, and unfortunately, that is sometimes the only way that systems are scrutinized and changes get done. But I'm going to take this question in a slightly different direction, and point to a phrase (not mine) that captures what I believe to be a huge and all too often unaddressed problem: the soft bigotry of low expectations.

Since 2002, NCLD has been awarding an annual scholarship to graduating high school seniors who have LD and who are poised to enroll in full-time four-year college study. One part of the application is a personal statement that asks about their journey through school and the impact LD has had on their classes, their extracurricular activities, and their involvement in the community. We've read dozens of essays where misinformation and stigma about LD almost derailed these talented, hard-working and highly accomplished students. We read about a debating coach who didn't think a student with dyslexia could compete with his peers (he went on to be a star on his college debate team). We learned about a guidance counselor who discouraged a student from applying to pharmacy school because she might make "spelling mistakes" when filling prescriptions. We just heard back from a young woman with LD who was told she should forget about trying to be a veterinarian (she graduated college and has successfully completed half of her vet school program; unfortunately she still needs to fight for needed accommodations.) The impact of stigma on these and so many individuals is undeniable. It's as though they are being judged and subjected to discrimination based on the misperception that LD is a prescription for underachievement.

Lawsuits are important because they test the ways laws work and they provide public proof that discrimination of any sort will not be tolerated. But thinking about these scholarship applicants, there is so much that society can and must do to protect people with LD from the stigma associated with low expectations. This is something that we can all do right now. Speaking out takes courage, but the alternative is to allow stigma to win.

Over the years, it seems like the stigma around dyslexia has decreased. I'd even say that lots of people wouldn't think twice about admitting they have dyslexia – but this seems to apply only to dyslexia, and possibly ADHD. Learning disabilities are another story. Do you agree?

I agree that the term "dyslexia" has become much more common over time and is being used more frequently than other terms such as "learning disabilities", "dyscalculia" (having to do with LD in math) and "dysgraphia" (which deals with writing). Learning disabilities is the overall umbrella term under which dyslexia and other types of LD fall, and is generally thought of as an educational classification. In contrast, dyslexia is a medical term that only recently is being recognized by the education community.

One of the reasons that the term dyslexia is better known than LD is that it has been the most studied area of education science during the past few decades. It also refers specifically to reading and literacy, and includes areas of skill development that are so critical to school performance and overall success in the workplace. Dyslexia is also a term that has been catapulted into public awareness by Hollywood celebrities, successful businessmen and entrepreneurs, scientists and others who have disclosed having dyslexia in very public ways. This is not the case for learning disabilities which, for the most part, remains the term used in education and civil rights law and one that needs further explanation to convey a person's specific areas of weakness.

Another reason might be the fact that the term "learning disabilities" does not mean the same thing in other parts of the world. For example, in the United Kingdom, LD refers to cognitive or intellectual disabilities (formerly referred to in the USA as mental retardation).

That said, the term "dyslexia" is not sufficient to describe the precise nature of a person's struggle. Some people with dyslexia have trouble decoding or sounding out words, others struggle with speed and fluency of reading, some with comprehension, written expression, spelling or a combination of these skills and more. It's important to remember that a significant number of people with LD (including dyslexia) have co-occurring ADHD, so their struggles may not be the result of a single disorder.

The bottom line is that greater public awareness of the terms "dyslexia," learning disabilities," and "ADHD" is a good thing, as long as it is coupled with accurate information and not associated with misinformation that can lead to stigma.

What would you say about the issue of using the terms learning difference vs. learning disability? When parents ask us this question, our standard response is that learning difference is fine,

though it's difficult to get services or government funding without the word disability. Is that still the case?

It is. No one is protected by special education law (the Individuals with Disabilities Education Act - IDEA) or civil rights law (the Americans with Disabilities Act- ADA) because they do anything 'differently'. Informal help is always available, but to be guaranteed services and supports in school, at work or in other settings, an individual needs to have a documented *disability* that impacts their life in a significant way.

Substituting the word "difference" for disability or disorder is definitely not a bad thing. It provides a different frame of reference that focuses not just on a person's struggles and allows for attention to be paid to the whole person. It acknowledges that they have areas of skill weakness but that they are just as capable as others if they are given the right kinds of accommodations and supports.

During the past decade, numbers of people, including some prominent researchers, have begun to talk about 'gift' of dyslexia or the 'benefits' of having LD or ADHD. These conversations have pointed to the unique abilities and strengths that some individuals with LD and ADHD have that appear to give them an edge over others when it comes to certain types of thinking and skill development. If we lived in a society where fast and accurate reading and writing was not the gold standard for success in school, we'd probably have many fewer people needing to be identified as having a disability. If you reflect upon the evolution of the human brain, and all the things that it needs to do, reading is the most recent of the challenges it has had to deal with. Written language is a fairly recent development (only a couple of thousands of years old) and it takes a very long time for human genetics and neurology to catch up with the rapidly changing demands of society. Of all the things we are wired to do, our brains are still learning how to deal with written language.

It's easy to see how the choice of terms we use relates to stigma. The phrases "my child has a learning disability" versus "my child learns differently" could carry different emotional weight, especially for a parent who is new to the world of LD. The same goes for using the terms "difference" and "disorder." My recommendation is that parents and individuals accept and embrace the specific terms that help them access the services and supports they need, when they need them, and for as long as they need them. Understanding the nature of their LD, being informed about their legal rights and opportunities, being confident in their ability to self-advocate for appropriate services and supports, and knowing their areas of strength as well as weakness are all ways to keep stigma out of the labeling equation.

My last question has to do with the stigma often associated with taking medication. We've heard from more than a few parents that they didn't want their child taking medication for ADHD. They knew that other kids with ADHD were helped by medication but were fearful of the potential side effects it might have on their child. And they even expressed a sense of shame and defeat, allowing their perceived stigma of needing medication to impact their decision. Is this common, and what advice would you offer to families like this?

Let me begin with the reminder that LD and ADHD are different types of disorders, and while many of their characteristics and symptoms may overlap, they are evaluated differently and require different types of intervention. We are fortunate that so much is known about ADHD and that there are carefully researched and well proven approaches to helping people who struggle with inattention, hyperactive and impulsivity. Ignoring good science and denying someone the treatment they need to enjoy success in school and in life is not something I would recommend. That said, ADHD is not like other medical conditions (like epilepsy or diabetes) where withholding medicine could result in significant physical harm. Turning to behavioral therapies rather than medication could work just fine, and a combination of medicine and behavioral approaches are likely to work even better. But the decision to take medicine is a personal one, and should be made only after open and honest discussion with all family members, (including the child!) and in close consultation with the doctor who will be prescribing the medicine and monitoring its effects.

How stigma comes into play has everything to do with how you see yourself as a person with ADHD. Thinking that having ADHD means you are "broken" in some way is an invitation for stigma to invade your thinking. Worrying about ADHD medication and imagining that it will increase your risk for addiction will strengthen stigma's grip and lead to unnecessary anxiety and shame. Understanding how medicine for ADHD works, knowing its possible side effects, being careful about how much to take and when, and knowing how to adjust to life activities on and off medicine (and when the effects of medicine are kicking in and tapering off) are the best ways to keep stigma in its place...far away!

STIGMA AND ADHD

A Conversation with Casey Dixon

When I wrote my second book, *On Their Own: Creating an Independent Future for Your Adult Child with Learning Disabilities and ADHD*, I wanted to include a chapter on Life Skills Coaching. This brought me to Casey Dixon, a Life Skills Coach based in Pennsylvania who specializes in helping those with Attention Deficit Disorder. She has intensified her focus in recent years toward helping lawyers and professors with their specific challenges brought on by their disabilities.

"Lawyers? Professors? How can this help my child?" you might ask.

Stigma knows no boundaries. It touches young and old, the educated and those with little education. If any lessons can be gleaned from this book, I hope the willingness to listen to others, to try to understand their experience, and to learn from them will be some of them.

Read Casey's insight into stigma as it has come into the lives of some we might not expect and see how very familiar much of it may be.

"My name is Casey Dixon. I'm an ADHD Life Coach and I specialize in working with adult professionals with ADHD. I have a highlight in my own practice working with lawyers and professors who have ADHD. I started coaching parents of kids with ADHD, but over time I found I was getting more and more calls from adults with ADHD. I was also getting more calls from people who were in more intellectual-heavy professions within academia and the law. It's really interesting to me, especially when it relates to the topic of stigma. There is an odd paradox that happens with people who are really smart and, on the surface, very successful. They've gotten their Ph.D., they're teaching at a research university, or they have their law degree and they're working in a law firm. On the surface, everything looks success-oriented but there is an undercurrent of struggle that comes with ADHD. How they deal with it from a stigma point of view is fascinating."

I asked Casey what is happening that propels her clients to seek out her help.

"As far as lawyers go, the American Bar Association came out with a study in 2016 that found attorneys reporting rates of ADHD at about 12.5%. That is about 2.5 times the number in the general adult population. Among these, I have two groups. I have the newer attorney who is a first or a third year associate and trying to develop their career. They are saying, 'Oh my goodness, I was able to pull out things at the last minute and do really well in law school, running on adrenalin. But now that I'm doing this job, it's not quite the same and I'm really struggling.' The second group tends to be in their mid-40s to mid-50s. They have gone through the first phase of their career and it still isn't feeling right or things aren't working the way they thought they would be by now. They're still struggling with managing their time or getting things organized and getting back to clients in a timely fashion. They also have family issues going on at the same time. They end up running on stress all the time."

"As for professors," I said, "I would think they love their profession."

"I think they do," Casey agreed, "but what I've found is that it can be very stressful when you're in that pre-tenure phase, when you have to produce a lot of writing while you're teaching classes and working with community-involvement on campus. You're transitioning from being a student and being told what to do, when to do it, and how to do it into someone in a position of being a teacher where you are the one responsible for deciding how to use your time. It requires a tremendous amount of self-regulation in terms of energy use and time management. It's pulling you in so many directions. That's when things start to fall apart for them. They love their job, but they're also thinking, 'I'm not getting anything done.'"

"Do you have a sense that they don't talk about it with anybody because they feel there is a stigma?"

"It's a pretty mixed bag. I have a couple of folks who say they don't care what people think. They believe that people already know they struggle with certain issues and they want to be able to tell them why they struggle. They want to tell them they have a diagnosis of ADHD. I had this conversation with a professor a couple of weeks ago. I was suggesting that she use some caution because she is a pre-tenure position. She says, 'I don't care what they think, I'm going to tell them the reason why I'm struggling.' I think most of the time when people disclose within their workplace, it's because they've gotten to a point where they just don't care. This can come from a point of being frustrated but it can also come from a point of being self-accepting. It's a really odd phenomenon."

"Unfortunately, when it comes to LD in the workplace," I said, "it doesn't matter if the Americans with Disabilities Act is there or not, there is still going to be some stigma involved and that can damage somebody's career."

"Oh, yes, definitely," Casey said. "That is why I always recommend extreme caution. With this particular professor, she is putting herself at risk. When you tell somebody who doesn't have ADHD and doesn't study ADHD that you have ADHD, they don't really understand it. You've just changed their lens on how they view everything you do as a professional."

"You could lose your job," I said.

"Yes, it's possible. You could lose your job or you could be really stuck within a non-growth position within an organization."

"This is stigma," I said. "It really is. The need to withhold divulging ADHD or LD within the workplace is a direct result of stigma. I always think of it as another arrow in the quiver if the employers are looking for a reason to keep you in the same place or ease you out of the company. We always recommend that someone should not disclose their disability unless it is directly affecting your job. This is not college or school in general, but specifically for employment situations. For instance, if you have a reading disability

141

but you don't have to read, why would you disclose it? You should probably lay low unless or until it becomes an issue. And again, this is all due to stigma. It's still there."

"It is still there."

"Now what about people who are not professionals who have come to you for help? Do you remember any stigma issues specific to them? Or is it the same?

"I think the workplace issues are a little bit different in terms of disclosure and legal issues and how to compensate for that. I am working with a mother now who is a stay-at-home mom. She's got five kids and she is really struggling with her ADHD. Three of her kids also have it. For her it's a family issue rather than a professional issue. It was really interesting what you said when we started is that you are looking at this from three different views: the self-stigma, the friends and family stigma, and then the workplace or societal stigma. I do see the self-stigma in nearly every one of my clients. This mom is very much struggling with her diagnosis. I always say to people that the path from diagnosis to acceptance of your disability is not a straight line. You're not going to go straight from, 'well, I got a diagnosis' to 'now I can accept that and feel good about who I am.'"

"Did she tell her children when she got the diagnosis?"

"Yes, she did. She told her family and she's working with them on setting up family systems to help all of them together. The problem is that she has a husband who is really put together and doesn't have any neurological issues. According to her, he is Mr. Perfect. She's always comparing herself to him."

"Is that how the self-stigma manifests itself?" I asked. "Beating herself up because she isn't as 'perfect' as he is?"

"Yes. There is a lot of shame involved in the self-stigma. One of the things I have seen is that the lower your power is within your family, organization or within society, the more you're apt to pile that on yourself. Because this woman does not have a lot of power and control in her life, she is there at the beck and call of her kids. I know that's what moms do a lot, but it's particularly true for her. And with her husband, she finds this a very shaming position. She'll go back and forth from self-acceptance to being self-critical."

"Is the husband critical of her? Or does she perceive that he is critical?"

"I don't think he's critical of her – but that's a rarity."

"Does she perceive that his being 'perfect' is some sort of comment on her own imperfections?"

"She perceives that in her position in her family and in society, she *should* be more perfect."

"I think when some people experience stigma, they see it where none actually exists. They may be wondering what people are thinking of them, when people might not be thinking anything."

"Absolutely true," Casey said. "This is something else I hear all the time: 'Everyone who doesn't have ADHD or dyslexia has such an easy life. They coast through work. They don't struggle with anything. Their finances are perfect and their family lives are harmonious.' Of course, while I'm listening, I'm also thinking...no."

"What do say to someone who says that to you?"

"That is what is called Black and White Thinking, or polarized thinking. I tell them, 'The reality is not that everybody else is perfect and you are flawed. Let's take a look at a little more gray area thinking. There may be tasks that you struggle with that are easier for your coworkers, but there are certain strengths that you have and we need to get back to talking about what those are. We need to talk about what is going right in your world'. A lot of it also depends on what they need at the moment. It may be we really need to look at where their life is going well so they can stop with the self-criticism, or it may be a specific problem they really are struggling with, and in that case, we need to attack it directly and look for a solution. It comes down to what is real and what is maladaptive thinking. That can be a really hard thing for someone to discover on their own. I think that is where working with a therapist or a life coach or a supportive friend who doesn't have an agenda can be extremely helpful. I talked to a man yesterday who was diagnosed with ADHD but he isn't really being treated. He has medication but he can't remember to take it. He called me and said the only reason he wants to go into coaching is that he's driving his wife crazy. They have two children, but she tells him she doesn't want three children – meaning she doesn't want to have to be watching over her husband like he's the third child. She sees every single thing he does through that lens of 'Well, it's your ADHD.'"

"That sounds like a problem," I said.

"It's a big problem. How is that man going to dig himself out of that? He does not have her support. She says things like, 'I'm not fixing that because I don't need three children.' He forgets to take his medication. He's not being treated with any other cognitive/behavioral interventions. He doesn't know how to find support. He doesn't know what to do. So he's stuck – and he's mired in self-stigma. He's starting to see his entire self through the lens of his neurological disorder, which is not a healthy place to be."

"I once met a man who told me he and his entire family had terrible ADHD," I said. "He said they get medication and it lasts for a while and they get their lives together, and then the medication stops working and their lives fall apart and they have to start all over again. It was such a cycle of difficulty. He had an attitude that it was pointless to really try to accomplish something with his life because he knew it would fall apart sooner or later. He limited himself."

"Sometimes self-limiting actions can be beneficial."

"How so?"

"You can't say yes to everything to please everybody in your life or you will be running around chaotically putting out fires all the time. That's a critical place to get to when you have ADHD. People with ADHD tend to be reactive to their external environment, so the other person's emergencies or their needs become more important than the needs of the person with the disability. They need to be realistic about what they can accomplish, with the knowledge that yes, it is going to be more difficult for them to sit down and write a dissertation than it might be for someone without ADHD. They might need more support than somebody else. I do think that's really important, as long as it's based on an incredibly high level of self-awareness and self-knowledge. If they just say, 'well, I have ADHD so I can't do anything,'...that's not helpful. They really need to get to a place where they are saying, 'well, I have ADHD so I need to be *extremely* intentional about what I do with my time and energy and talent.'"

"In our book *On Their Own*, you told us about a CEO of a company who had ADHD. You said he had all these major responsibilities, yet he was out in the hallway changing a light bulb."

"Yes! That is a good example. He probably had a stack of things that he was avoiding on his desk and his ADHD brain made it easier for him to say, 'oh, something else needs to be done, I'm going to go do it. It doesn't matter whether its part of my job or the most valuable use of my time – it's in my face, so it's going to get done.' The whole societal view of ADHD has changed a lot. The more that people come out and tell us they have ADHD and they are also successful in their career, the more helpful that would be. But we must remember, the people who are divulging in the media are coming from positions of power. They are CEOs and Olympic athletes and movie stars and people at the top of their careers. Those famous successful people who talk about having ADHD or dyslexia don't really have anything to risk by coming out and talking about it. They're still going to have their success. But it affects people who aren't famous and are just getting up and going to work and trying to get dinner on the table and remembering to put their car keys in the right place at the end of the day. It's the everyday things, paying bills and picking up kids from school, the everyday things of normal life that can give them trouble. It's important for them to have exemplars in the media who say they have ADHD and I'm still successful, but it can also create a very unfortunate dichotomy, in which people say, 'Well, if that person can do that and they have ADHD, then what is wrong with me? I'm still struggling so hard on a day to day basis just to live.'"

I said, "As far as stigma goes with these adults, we seem to have the two types: the person who thinks of themselves in a negative way, which is self-stigma. Or those who are facing some sort of genuine stigma in the workplace. In your opinion, which is more prevalent and which is worse?"

"I would say the internal self-stigma is the most powerful in terms of how much damage it can do to the person."

"How do you help them overcome it? You already mentioned the Black and White thinking? Is there anything else you would suggest?"

"I think it's important to find out how they view their own disorder, because technically it is a disorder. Do they think it's real? I'm working with a college student now and he tells me that he doesn't think ADHD is real. Of course, I'm thinking 'you're sitting here at ADHD coaching, what is that about?' He said he would rather be known as lazy."

"What in the world is he thinking?" I asked. "He doesn't want to have the stigma of ADHD, but he'd rather have the stigma of 'lazy'?"

"Yes. For him, lazy is cool. A neurological disorder is not cool. As life coaches, with every single person, we need to be extremely careful to discover where the root of that stigma lies for each individual. Is it the way their husband or wife or partner is approaching a situation? Is it something that's going on at work? Is it something like this college student is saying, that he'd rather be known as lazy than as having ADHD? Are they in denial about their diagnosis or don't think it's real?"

"How did it end up with you and that student?"

"I have to respect where he is and meet him at that place. I have to say, 'if it's not called ADHD, what is it you need to focus on? If you don't want to call it ADHD, what do you want to call it?' He comes back and tells me he needs some help with time management. And so we'll do that, we'll focus on it as time management challenges. In that case, I'm not going to convince him that ADHD is real, so there's no point in spending time on that. With a lot of my clients, we really need to start with them learning how to be an advanced user of ADHD. For instance, if I'm dyslexic or I have ADHD, I need to know what that means. I need to know how to use it."

"It sounds like another way of saying self-advocacy," I said. "We always push for parents to teach their children how to advocate for themselves. The same would go for an adult with LD or ADHD. The first thing they all need to do is understand what they have."

"Exactly. You can't ask for what you need unless you know what it is."

"We often hear learning differences as opposed to learning disabilities," I said.

"The problem with that – and this is just my opinion – but because I spend all day working with people who are really struggling in their daily lives because of their diagnosis or symptoms of ADHD, I see that it really is a disabling condition. It's so much more than a simple difference. We have to be very careful with this. A lot of my clients are not getting appropriate treatment, which makes them throw up their hands and say, 'well, I guess I'm just different,' because there is no real solution for this. If I was diabetic, it would be really clear what course of treatment I need to follow. But it is not clear with ADHD, and doctors often don't know what they're doing. I think the medical professionals are contributing to the stigma because they are ignorant of what this disorder really is and how to treat it. In fact, I went to my own family physician a couple months ago for my annual checkup. He's always curious about my job. He asks me about it every time. Last time he said, 'do you really think ADHD is real?' How is that even plausible? These are our doctors! They have the power to do the diagnosis and to medicate people and to treat people for this, and then he asks me if I believe it's real. I built my whole career on it, so obviously I think it's real! I think it is really irresponsible to ask me that question. He's the physician. Go find out what the research is saying. It won't take very long to discover that question is just absurd and that it isn't based on science. It's based on your own weird belief."

"It's stigma," I said.

"Yes, it is. And all the research is consistent. We know it's not caused by kids having too much sugar or watching too much television. Even with adults, the stigma is huge. For them, it might not be thought a result of bad parenting, or too much sugar, or too many video games. Instead it's a lack of willpower, a lack of character, or not being smart enough. It's that same old script that these people have been hearing all their lives and, sometimes, they are saying it to themselves. And no wonder. If they go the doctor and the doctor has that viewpoint, it will be very difficult for that person to find the appropriate help."

I asked Casey if she had any concluding thought about stigma and the ways people can try to overcome it or deal with it in their lives.

"First of all," she said, "they should become more self-aware and more knowledgeable about their own challenges and their own strengths and their own interests, and try to accept that and stick with that. It's really hard. You can be accepting of it one minute and then next minute you can be so frustrated with it, you only wish it would go away. It's a circular process that we need to keep returning to. I do it with my clients. I also think really focusing on a strength-based approach is important. That's starting to sound cliché, but it really does help. It doesn't help completely. We can't just say, 'oh, focus on what you're good at.' We all live in a world where we have to be good at many, many different things. We can't easily say we only want to be good at one thing."

"Focusing on the strengths really can help self-esteem," I said.

"It certainly does help, and I think it's really important to really highlight and shine a bright light on those strengths. I'll give a good example. I have a professor I work with who has dyslexia and ADHD. She teaches at a large research university and she hates herself because she didn't get her syllabus for her class turned in on time. Does she need to work on that time-management issue? Yes, she does. She needs to have her syllabus turned in at some point, and it would be easier if we can figure out a way to make that process more efficient for her. So that's focusing on her weakness. But while we're doing that, we need to really shine a light on the fact that she's got graduate students coming from all over the world to that university to study with her. She is a top expert in her field. She is working for the United Nations. So yes, she has dyslexia and ADHD and she has trouble with deadlines and she is constantly frustrated with herself, but look at the gifts she gives to the world and the strengths she brings to her organization and her family. It's just staggering. I have to keep going back to tell her to take a look at those things to remind her of those gifts and not be constantly challenge-focused. I call it self-improvement mania. You get a diagnosis of ADHD. Now you have to 'fix it', but it may not be fixable. What you need to do is learn how to live your best life within the parameters you have. It's a different approach. I try to help my clients see that this is not something you just fix and forget. It's something you will have to relearn about and renegotiate all the time."

"That's a great way of looking at it because the reality is; they are going to have to deal with it. And how do they do that? That's the important thing. How do you learn to live a happy life with your disability?"

"That's right. And learning to do that goes a long way in helping get past the stigma."

ADDING FUEL TO THE STIGMA FIRE

Additional Concerns for Parents

I have chosen four topics I wanted to include in this book, as each one can lead to further stigma on top of that already faced by children and adults with LD.

They are:

- Obesity
- Substance Abuse
- Social Media,
- Problems with Social Skills (probably the most important one of all).

I have touched upon these concerns in other books I have written and speeches I have given to various parent groups because they come up over and over again. Experience tells me these four subjects are not often talked about in relation to LD (except, perhaps, social skills as this is a problem that is direct and obvious and can cause great distress for parents and children alike).

What I don't understand is that there is very little information for parents on some of these topics, especially obesity and substance abuse in relation to LD. As you'll see, when I wrote about substance abuse and LD, I had to rely on a report I was involved with creating back in September 2000. These topics might not be discussed in professional settings, but when you put any group of parents together, these are the sorts of things they most want to talk about.

OBESITY AND STIGMA

S ome experts have told me there is no correlation between obesity and learning disabilities. I'm not sure I agree with this. Special needs and obesity do not *necessarily* go together, but I have seen enough first-hand evidence to tell me that they *often* go together.

This is a delicate topic because we all know that obesity among all Americans is at epidemic levels. Anyone can have this trouble. Some parents who read this may think they would have a difficult time discussing the subject with their child as they, too, have their own challenges with weight. Children with and without disabilities are affected. Our former First Lady Michelle Obama tried her best to fight obesity in young people but with limited success. It is not uncommon to pass a McDonald's after school lets out and see the same group of high school students, day after day, socializing while they feast on high-calorie fast food.

Weight gain and obesity among those with LD doesn't quite make the radar screen of many experts. I cannot find a lot of information linking the two. What I can find, however, are parents who insist this is a major concern. I well remember a conversation I had with a mother in Connecticut whose child was living in a group home for similar young adults with special needs. "Thank you so much for talking about this," she said. "No one else will. The school officials tell us there is nothing wrong, but we parents are up in arms because the food being served at the home is all junk food and high in calories. There's no organization or discipline, and no effort to teach them about how to eat in a healthy way. And this is the trouble: some of our kids have no concept of health or the effects of junk food on their bodies. They're all twenty or thirty pounds overweight. Sometimes even more. We parents have organized to go to the residence officials and demand they start addressing this problem."

Let's for a moment leave aside the normal teenage tendency to indulge in junk food and sugary snacks. Let's also leave aside the fact that some people simply don't care about weight gain. The ones I'm concerned about are those whose LD leaves them completely unequipped to figure out a way to manage their eating habits. Let's say you have a daughter who has left home for the first time and is attending a college with a strong support system for students with LD. Maybe she has gained a few pounds. You, or her friends, or even a nutritionist may explain food labels to her, and assume that is all it takes. But is it? Imagine having dyscalculia (learning disabilities that involve math) and trying to figure out the numbers on a label. It is a daunting task.

The Center for Disease Control states that one thirds of adults in the United States – more than 72 million people – are obese. The CDC also states that children and adults with mobility limitations and intellectual or learning disabilities are at *greatest risk* for obesity.

Let's look at some reasons why a child or adult with LD or ADHD might have difficulty maintaining weight.

The magazine *ADDvance* conducted a survey of adult women with ADD about their eating habits. The survey indicated a great deal of trouble with compulsive over-eating or binge eating. Many of the respondents said they used food, especially carbohydrates such as bread, starchy foods or sweets as a way to calm down or to self-medicate. Surely we can all relate to this. We've had a stressful day, maybe we didn't have a chance to eat a proper meal, and now we're home, ready to unwind. Do we cook a healthy meal of a salad, followed by a broiled chicken breast and vegetables? Of course not! We reach for the macaroni and cheese, especially the kind that doesn't require too much work.

But what if *every* day is stressful, and not only because of outside influences like a project deadline or a demanding work schedule, but because you bring the source of stress with you wherever you go in the form of LD or ADHD? What if simple acts taken for granted by most others become a daily source of anxiety? In these cases, the occasional self-medicating dose of comfort food may become a daily fixture, and with it comes the added pounds and expanding waistline.

"I know LD has a lot to do with my daughter Marie's weight problems," one mother told me. "In fact, I think it has *everything* to do with it. Marie seems to have no sense of balance. She doesn't appear to have a self-image like many other teenagers. I know other teenage girls who are overweight, but at least they *know* they're overweight. Marie seems to be unaware of her situation, and doesn't seem to comprehend the link between over-eating and obesity. And of course there is also the stigma. She is not only stigmatized because she has LD and is in special ed, she is also stigmatized because of her weight."

And here we go, circling around to the subject of this book.

Stigma is always lurking around those with disabilities. The same can be said for those who have weight problems.

A recent article in the *New York Times*, entitled *Fat Bias Starts Early and Takes a Serious Toll* says "obesity has become the last socially acceptable form of prejudice, and persons with obesity are considered acceptable targets of stigma....furthermore, experiencing weight stigma can result in a poor self-image, depression, and stress; and that, in turn, increases the risk of poor eating habits and difficulty losing weight. People can internalize weight stigma, blaming themselves for their excess weight and the social discrimination they experience."

I was in an elevator at an event for a learning disabilities organization and was talking about this book with a friend. A woman overheard our conversation and stopped me in the lobby of the hotel. "My son has LD and faces a lot of stigma," she told me, "but I would honestly say that the stigma is not at all centered on the fact that he has LD but because he's overweight. That's where all the trouble comes in. He has no friends and no social life, and it's all because of his poor self-image due to his weight."

When I asked her if she has tried to help him, she told me she does what she can, "but that's where his LD comes into play," she said. "He simply cannot figure out the realities of nutrition or how to eat properly. I try to help, but I can't be with him all the time. He has poor impulse control. He has good intentions, but they all fall by the wayside when a pizza arrives."

Allegra had similar troubles a couple of times in her life. Her case is unusual in that she spent so much time skating that she never had to worry about it; but during those times when she hasn't been as active on the ice or at the gym, she has experienced what so many other Americans do. The skirt "suddenly" doesn't fit any more. The jeans can't be buttoned. Unlike Marie, Allegra is very aware of her appearance. She might not know all the details of nutrition and a healthy diet, but she certainly understands that jeans that can no longer be buttoned did not suddenly shrink on their own. Even so, the first time it happened I was concerned when I saw no sign that she was trying to change.

I decided to talk to her about it. This is always a risky thing. No one wants to hear about how much weight they have gained, and I didn't know how Allegra would take it. We went out to dinner one night and I tried to keep the conversation light. In the middle of our talk I said, "I've noticed that you've gained a little weight." Before she could respond I followed up with, "I have too, and I just wanted you to know that I can help you with it. We can help each other."

Luckily my observation did not come as a surprise. Allegra was more than happy to let me help her.

After she went back home we faxed menus back and forth to each other. Nothing formal or typed out, just hand-written lists of what she planned to have for dinner. We sometimes did it by phone or email. The trick is to make it fun and a challenge – an *easy* challenge. There's no point in turning the act of eating into a chore, nor will it help to insist that your child follow a diet based on rice cakes and lettuce. Moderation and knowledge are the answers.

There are very good programs out there such as Weight Watchers, Nutri-system, and Jenny Craig (I am most familiar with Weight Watchers as I have friends who follow their program, but many thousands of people have met with success with each of them.)

Some of these program consist of weekly meetings and a method to track and control weight. Leaders are extremely accommodating and understanding, and will undoubtedly go out of their way to assist any child or adult with LD. It is certainly worth your time to go to one of these centers near you to talk to someone about your child and to see if this might be a viable way to help get their weight under control. Our children with LD already have enough challenges with stigma. We must try, if at all possible, to help them avoid the stigma that comes with too much weight.

ALCOHOL AND SUBSTANCE ABUSE

Having a learning disability or related disorders is difficult enough. Now add the problem of alcohol or drug abuse, and you can create a firestorm of stigma.

Let's start with a young man who experienced these problems first hand. "I drank a lot and I also smoked marijuana because it helped alleviate the hyperactivity of ADHD," he told me. "It helped calm my nerves and allowed me to study. I would smoke a joint and sit in the same place and write an entire paper. Basically I was self-medicating. It caused a huge amount of trouble. The marijuana takes away motivation. Even now I'm around a lot of big shots with my work and I feel so small compared to them. I would never mention drinking or marijuana around them because they wouldn't understand. They came from an environment that was completely different. There is a stigma against the things I did. My self-medicating helped in some ways, but it ended up causing many more problems. The drinking caused even more trouble than the marijuana. I had to stop doing both, but then the ADHD flares up. I've had a hard time keeping a job because I say things....for instance, I'll be in a meeting and I'll just blurt stuff out. I feel vulnerable because I'm constantly open to attack from other employees, especially in a corporate environment. You're vulnerable if you have ADHD. You reveal things about yourself that you shouldn't. You say things that you shouldn't. It's hard for me to sit at my desk and actually work. There are errors in my emails. I forget to do things. It's a constant battle. All my life, in high school

157

and college, I've had to work 150% harder just to be 80% as good as the normal students. When I was using marijuana and drinking, it didn't seem so bad. But like I said, that behavior led to even more troubles."

The temptation to escape the pain, the frustration, and the stigma (whether real or not) is never far away for teenagers and young adults with LD and related disorders. *Escape* seems to be the word most often used by them. This doesn't always mean they'll turn to substance abuse to do this: some may immerse themselves in video games, for instance, and before long that will overwhelm all other aspects of their lives. For others, the need for friends and the sense of belonging to a group will compel them into the "wrong crowd" where the only requirement for inclusion is the desire to drink or smoke and escape from the real world for a time.

Let's be clear about this: nearly every teenager will experiment with one thing or another at some point. My concern is for those who go beyond this common rite-of-passage type of behavior.

When I was Chairman of the National Center for Learning Disabilities, I was asked by Joseph Califano, Chairman of the Center on Addiction and Substance Abuse (CASA) at Columbia University to speak at a seminar on the link between substance abuse and learning disabilities. Both Joe and I felt this was an issue that was not adequately covered and to this day, seventeen years later, our report is still the one cited in nearly every article on this subject.

Our report was called *Substance Abuse and Learning Disabilities: Peas in a Pod or Apples and Oranges?* (You can download the report by visiting the website of the National Center on Addiction and Substance Abuse (www.centeronaddiction.org) and searching for learning disabilities, or downloading the report directly from this web address: https://www.centeronaddiction.org/addiction-research/reports/substance-abuse-learning-disabilities)

Nobody has come up with a direct, provable link between learning disabilities and substance abuse, such as a gene or other scientific marker, but I have personally seen a link in many families. The fact is, behavioral effects of LD are also risk factors for substance abuse. These include low self-esteem, poor school performance, depression, peer-rejection, problems reading social cues in groups, loneliness and the desire for social acceptance.

Every one of these risk factors can lead to a young adult seeking out relief. I have friends in recovery from alcoholism who tell me they first began to drink because it was a social lubricant. It lessened the anxiety of being a teenager and helped them become more popular, less insecure, the life of that party. That usually lasted until the party became such a problem they had no choice but to put an end to it.

I don't believe individuals with LD have a specific genetic risk of substance abuse, but I do believe they have social challenges (very much including stigma) that lead them to see alcohol and drugs as the answer to their prayers. It's a terrible, vicious cycle: the stigma of LD leads to substance abuse, which in turn brings its own stigma, which throws more fuel on the stigma fire, which leads to more destructive behavior.

Let's take the desire for social acceptance as an example. I know of a young woman who had no friends in high school. She had no social life at all. In order to have even one friend, she forced her way into that ever-present "wrong crowd" and began first to use drugs, and then to sell them. This was her way of creating what she perceived as a social life and finding acceptance amongst her peers. Astoundingly (to me), she did this with her parents' knowledge. I can't say they supported it, but they knew about it. In their minds and in the mind of their daughter, *any* friend – even one in these circumstances where the so-called friends were simply using this girl for their own addictions – was better than a life alone.

Peer-pressure and the desire to be popular are very powerful in a teenager's life.

Parents really need to be on top of this, and pay attention, and talk to you're their children. They should also remember this: you are not their friend, you are a parent. As with the overweight parent who is afraid to discuss their child's weight, some parents will think, "How can I say something to my son? I was just like him. I smoked marijuana when I was his age."

Well, yes. So? Because you did something does not mean you have to turn a blind eye when your children do it. It is hypocrisy, no question about it. It is "Do as I say, not as I do." It is all those things – but did you also have learning disabilities that brought their own challenges with social skills and academics? Can you say that your own use of substances would have seemed "normal" if you coupled it with the stigma and day-to-day troubles experienced by your child with LD?

We parents have an awesome responsibility. We must try to protect and guide our children through the teenage years with all their attendant problems and temptations, while allowing them freedom at the same time.

We must be particularly vigilant when it comes to our children with LD. They already have so many elements of the very things that lead to substance abuse.

Many believe that addiction is a moral problem and those who suffer the addictions, even those who are in recovery, are blamed by society for causing their own problems. This blame creates additional stigma, which creates shame, guilt and fear, which prevents many from getting the treatment they need.

There are many organizations that focus on helping people recover from alcoholism and substance abuse. The most well-known among them, Alcoholics Anonymous, has been around since 1935 and has helped millions of people throughout the world live sober lives. It is a 12-step program, in that it has formulated twelve steps that help lead a person to their goal of sobriety, and it is the inspiration for every other twelve-step program such as NA (Narcotics Anonymous), OA (Overeaters Anonymous), and GA (Gamblers Anonymous).

Both AA and NA provide support for teenagers who may feel they have no one who understands what they are experiencing. If you as a parent feel there is an issue, try to talk to someone at your local AA Intergroup (the referral and information service manned by AA volunteers). You can find the contact information for your state on their AA website: www.aa.org. There are thousands of meetings throughout the United States every single day, and someone will be able to explain the program and give advice on how to help your child (or you!).

SOCIAL MEDIA AND LEARNING DISABILITIES

In today's world, social skills are not confined to face-to-face interactions. More and more children and adults are engaging in frequent (sometimes too frequent) communications online. Not only are there no face-to-face interactions, but sometimes there is no face at all. We've all heard frightening stories of the online stalker who hides behind an assumed identity and the identity-thief who gains access to your most personal matters.

Children and young adults *without* LD can get into trouble online, but what happens when you add learning disabilities to the mix? Imagine a child who has trouble with social skills and has trouble making friends. These lonely children are often desperate to find that one classmate or friend who will spend time with them and pay attention to them. They are vulnerable and may leap at the chance to chat online with their new best friend (who they have never seen, have no idea how old this friend is, and cannot say for sure what this friend's true name is.)

Due to my daughter's age, I never had to go through the fears and worries faced by parents of today's internet generation, and can only imagine what it is like. How can you stop it? Is it even possible to stop it? Is it desirable to stop it completely? Our society has become one of (mostly) young people staring at a screen. They do it at home, they do it in school, they stare while walking down the street. Some risk their lives by doing it while driving. Texting, surfing the web, chatting, posting on Facebook: the world has opened up in ways we once could never have imagined while, at the same time, has become less friendly, with less direct interpersonal communication and less community overall.

Trying to stop this is like trying to stop the tide. It is going to happen whether we like it or not. Instead, we need to find ways to monitor the online activities of the most vulnerable among us to be sure things do not go too far off-track.

Parents of younger children and pre-teens should be very careful and attempt to know the sites their children are visiting online. There are technologies that can help them with that. As an example, I found an app called Circle that pairs with your home Wi-fi to let you manage every device on your network. You can set time limits for apps and websites. You can also set up appropriate filters to prevent your child from getting onto inappropriate websites. Don't feel guilty about acting like a helicopter parent over this. There are times when helicopters are useful.

Different (but no less serious and hurtful) problems can come from popular and supposedly innocent social media sites such as Snapchat, Instagram and Facebook. The potential for online bullying is huge. It doesn't even have to be a direct and aggressive type of bullying to have an effect. Picture here a child with LD who goes onto Facebook and discovers every one of his classmates at a weekend party he was not invited to attend.

One mother told me a story about her son with severe LD. For some reason, he started to misplace things, and not small things like a key or a small toy truck. Big things, like his new mountain bike. His allowance mysteriously disappeared too. When pressed, he admitted that he hadn't lost his bike but had given it away to a new "friend" he met online. When the mother asked him to show her his new friend on Facebook, she discovered it was a local boy a couple of years older who ended up selling the bike before she could get it back (I never did hear how the thief made reparations, but I do remember the mother telling me her son was upset that she interfered with this newfound "friendship.")

These kids are so desperate for companionship they will latch onto anybody who speaks to them. Again – do not feel as if you are being overly intrusive when you take a look into your child's online life. Think of it this way: if your child had friends over and they were playing in your living room, would you feel intrusive by sticking your head into the room to see who was there and if everything was going smoothly? Probably not. Think of online activity the same way.

When it comes to teenagers, I leave it up to your discretion. You know your child better than anyone. Is he or she mature enough to be left to their own devices? Are they able to properly judge the motives of others they meet online? When Allegra began to go online I had already seen enough proof that she was a fairly keen judge of character. I still hovered a bit, but not in overt, intrusive ways.

The Internet is not all bad news. It can also open our children's lives to entirely new worlds and positive new ways of learning and communicating. When Allegra was in her thirties, she only truly wanted one thing: to be in a relationship. After a couple of false starts, she discovered (on her own) an online dating site. I confess I nearly had a heart attack when she told me about it, but she was in her thirties. I felt I could not come right out and forbid it. That wouldn't have worked: I had spent so many years trying to give Allegra the ability to live an independent life, and now that she was showing true independence, I couldn't very well put an end to it. I had to accept it. At the same time, I wasn't about to sit back and do nothing. I looked into the online company and discovered it was a reputable site that pre-screened all the members.

I weighed the pros and cons. On the pro side of things, I saw it as a safe alternative to going out to bars or clubs. When a young adult has significant troubles with social skills, meeting someone in a formal, supervised online way could be viable and safe. On the con side, I had to overcome my own fears, which were entirely based on my unfamiliarity with this new form of social interaction. There was also the chance she would meet someone I didn't approve of – but my goodness, that could happen no matter where and how she met the "man of her dreams". (I should add that she was more successful than I could have imagined. She met an absolutely wonderful young man and they have been together ever since, now living as husband and wife.)

Social media has been a very big plus in Allegra's life. She interacts with friends every day on Facebook. She emails on a regular basis. She takes advantage of every holiday to use the Internet to send messages to everyone she knows.

That is the positive side of online life. Now let's look a little more closely at some of the negative.

Cyberbullying

Ty Tashiro in his book *Awkward* talks about people who have great difficulties in social situations. He says, "The Internet has helped awkward people form friendships founded on special interests, but the Internet may also harm human connections because many of the social cues humans have relied on for thousands of years are absent online." There's no question this is the same for people with LD.

I expect most parents' greatest fear regarding the internet is that their child will be lured into a meeting with an adult sexual predator. This is a genuine fear and certainly does happen, but far more children fall victim to online bullying, or cyber-bullying, by classmates and contemporaries than predatory adults.

Parents and teachers are usually aware of classroom or playground bullying and can take direct action to put an end to it. Online bullying is different. It often cannot be seen by parents or responsible adults. It happens in Instagram and Snapchat and other sites we adults do not always understand (and even if we do understand them, we are often not welcome in those secretive worlds. It is well-known that teenagers tend to shy away from Facebook once they discover their grandmother has the ability to make embarrassing comments on what they are wearing).

The sad, tragic truth is that a small number of children are so tormented by online bullying and harassment that they see no other way out but suicide – imagine how heart-wrenching this must be for the parent who had no idea the bullying was happening at all.

Many parents have absolutely no idea of the extent of their child's online activities. You may think you do – but do you? Do you understand Snapchat? Have you even heard of the latest site that is all the rage? I know for a fact that some of the teenagers of my acquaintances rarely use their phone as an actual device to talk to another person. One teenage girl I know is on her phone all day, every day, and yet her mother told me she clocked in only *two minutes* in one entire month on an actual phone call. With her, it is all texting, private messages, mysterious communications, and photos that disappear thirty seconds after posting.

Rather than hoping to put a stop to online bullying during or after it happens, parents should make an effort to prepare their child to deal with a bullying situation *before* it happens.

Parents must gain a clear-eyed understanding of the particular online risks faced by children with special needs.

The first step is to explain to the child what online bullying is. Some may not realize that is what is going on. Ask your child if he or she has been called names (or worse) online. Some children with LD may not actually recognize bullying for what it is. They may not understand the words used, or the subtlety of some remarks. If it's not too intrusive, maybe you, the parent, can have access to some of the sites to monitor what is going on (up until at least the teen years, I think all parents *should* monitor their child's online activities.)

One form of bullying that can really hurt a child with LD is the one I mentioned earlier: social isolation and the realization that everyone but your child is invited to a party or event. With every school function plastered all over the web, it would be easy to feel left out, and easy to be purposely made to feel left out. An official school activity will probably not result in your child being excluded, but small cliques of children and, especially, teens can develop within those activities, and those most definitely can find ways to exclude those they feel do not "belong".

Because of the challenges with friendship, children with special needs are more prone to gullibility. They may be so eager to develop a friendship that they will connect with the wrong crowd or fall victim to humiliating online practical jokes. They may send an embarrassing picture of themselves to an online bully who will then gleefully and maliciously share it with classmates. There are so many pitfalls!

Once again, it is crucial for parents to monitor young children's online presence and to do as much as you can with your older children – talk to them, ask them questions, do not let them suffer in silence. If you discover any sort of bullying, bring it to the attention of the school. As painful as it might be, there is a possibility that some parents will discover their own child is the bully. If that happens, put a stop to it at once. Do not fall into "he doesn't understand" reasoning – *make* him understand.

This is a bewildering world for some parents but it is our duty to make an effort to understand it.

PROBLEMS WITH SOCIAL SKILLS

What do we mean by "problems" with social skills? First, we can assume that a child's lack of friends does not come about simply because they have learning disabilities. It usually involves their difficulties with social skills. While some of their classmates might notice they attend special ed classes, or have trouble reading, most (but not all) children will not use that as the main reason to avoid playing with that child. After all, how much reading will they do on the basketball court or on the playground? The real troubles come in when a child cannot fit in and when normal every-day interactions take on a strange and unexpected quality – a great example is one I used earlier when recounting my experiences with Allegra as a child who could not understand the rules to what everyone else saw as a simple game. For those other children, the inability of a contemporary or older playmate to figure out an obvious set of rules is both strange and unexpected. They wonder why the older child can't figure this out.

I believe a lack of social skills leads to more stigma than any other behavior associated with LD. If you can't read, there are ways of getting around it. If you can't have a conversation without causing confusion and disruption, that can lead to real problems.

A friend of mine told me about her grandson Matthew's troubles with friendship. "One night I went in his room to chat with him," she said. "It was Halloween and I was curious why he wasn't out trick-or-treating with friends. What he told me was so painful, I wrote it all down."

I asked her why she did that and she told me she thought it might be useful someday when his parents were talking to school officials about challenges he faced due to LD.

Here is what she wrote:

On Halloween night, I went into Matthew's room about 8:30 p.m. to ask if he wanted anything.

"No thanks, Nana," he said, sitting at his computer. After a pause he added: "I am here alone on Halloween night and it sucks. Everyone else is at a party."

I sat beside him on the bed. "How do you know that?"

"I just know it."

"But how, Matthew?"

He swiveled his laptop and showed me a series of pictures on Instagram. They all showed groups of laughing, happy teenagers at a Halloween party that very night. They were Matthew's classmates. "I have no friends, Nana," he said. "Did I ever have friends?"

"There was Josh," I reminded him. "You guys used to sing and laugh in the back of the car whenever I drove you to school."

He nodded as if remembering how they sparred and laughed. "But that was then, and Josh moved away," he said. "It's different now. I'm awkward, Nana. I don't know how to talk to anyone. I see classmates in the hall that I want to talk to but I'm too scared. When I do try to talk to someone, I talk too much and they aren't interested. It's so painful. I hate it. I look at people and then avoid them because I don't know what to say. They are all gossiping but since I don't know anyone, I don't have anything to talk about. I'm so awkward."

"Well, the way to make friends is through sports teams and clubs" I said.

"The clubs are during school and I do my homework during school because I don't want to do my homework at home. I'm lazy."

I tried not to say much for I realized Matthew was sharing his vulnerability. "Well, there must be some guys in cross-country you like," I said. "What about your other teammates?"

"I texted two tonight. One was going to the Halloween party. The other one has no plans."

"Why don't you get together with him?" I suggested. "He's probably sitting at home right now, just like you."

"I don't know how to do that, Nana. I don't know how to ask people to do things. If they don't invite me, I don't know how to do it. That's why I don't have any friends."

"Who would you like to be friends with?" I asked. "Have you identified anyone you would like as a friend?"

"Yes, two seniors. But if I become their friends, they'll graduate and I'll have no friends again."

"Are there any classes where you have teams to work on projects? That's how people become friends, by working together."

"I have a partner in French but I can't ask her to do anything because it will look like I was asking her to be my girlfriend. If there was another guy with us, maybe I could ask her to do something."

This conversation went on for twenty minutes, the grandmother remembers. "This is how I remember it," she said when she handed me her notes. "I am quoting his statements. They were painful to hear. We ended the conversation and I suggested he should invite a few people over to play ping-pong, watch a movie and eat pizza."

"And did he do that?"

"No. It never happened."

This grandmother's heartache is so common to parents of children with LD. When I look back at Allegra's childhood, the things that cause me the most pain have nothing to do with school. There were some painful school episodes, to be sure, but the ones that still cause me to cringe when I think of them all had to do with socialization – or, rather, a lack of it. That terrible feeling I had when the phone rang and she answered it, fully expecting it to be one of the young girls she had invited over to play…and it never was. Seeing her alone in her room, talking to her dolls. Seeing her befriend an older woman during our summer vacations because no one her age would come over to play – or, if they did come over, would only do it once.

I have never been able to shake off these memories. Even now they affect me, even though she now has a full social life and true friends. If I think about it, I become sad all over again

So back to my question: what do we mean by "problems with social skills"? Here are some classic examples of behavior or traits that lead to challenges in friendships.

- Talking too much, or too loud, or too close (people have a sense of their "space," and when someone intrudes upon that space, it can be very uncomfortable).

- Not knowing boundaries (asking inappropriate questions or assuming a level of friendship that is not there.) Rick Lavoie, former headmaster at one of Allegra's schools, the Riverview School on Cape Cod, called this "putting out the candle of friendship." These children will become so possessive of any new friend and so afraid of losing that friend; they will go overboard and drive them away. They don't want to share the friend and if, for instance, they see that friend talking to someone else, it can cause a huge crisis. "We call it putting out the candle," Rick said, "because they light the candle of friendship and then put it out by being overly possessive."

- Impulsivity, saying whatever comes to mind without filtering. For instance, "This is so boring," when a child has come over to play.

- Not understanding social cues, facial cues, etc.

- Not understanding humor.

- Not making eye contact. When a person does not make eye contact during a conversation, it can be very disconcerting. Many people with LD will look at the ceiling, the floor, or even close their eyes when in conversation. Many people without LD do this, of course, but it's particularly prevalent in those with Asperger's Syndrome.

- Poor judgment, with little thought about logical consequences.

- Immaturity and "bossy" behavior. (I have seen this in action between two sisters. The one without LD often invited friends over. The older sister with LD became extremely bossy to an extent that her sister never again invited her friends to their house.)

- Self-centeredness. So many of these children have had so much attention given to them by their parents, that they become self-absorbed. This is such a problem that it sometimes comes up as the first topic of conversation when speaking to teachers at a special school. "They are so egotistical," one told me. "I can't break through to her to help her think about anything outside herself. It causes a lot of friction with her classmates."

One type of learning disability that has been linked to troubles with social skills is NVLD, or non-verbal learning disabilities. When I first heard this term, I assumed it meant the person had trouble with verbal expression, or perhaps, could not talk at all, but non-verbal LD means the person has difficulty understanding social cues that are not verbal. For instance, they may not be able to "read" another person's facial expressions or body language. They may have difficulty understanding the subtleties of language, and sarcasm, jokes or exaggeration may be taken literally. There is a bit of overlap with Asperger's Syndrome, though NVLD and Asperger's are separate conditions (and individuals with Asperger's tend to have much greater troubles with social skills).

Here are some of the symptoms of NVLD:

- Physically uncoordinated, awkward
- Thinks in literal terms (doesn't "get" humor, sarcasm)
- Is overly dependent on parents and other adults (prefers to interact with adults rather than children their own age)
- Dependent on routine, trouble adjusting to any changes.

"I Don't Know What to Do."

Those are the words most parents end up with at the end of a long effort to improve their child's social skills. Matthew's grandmother touched upon so many flashpoints in her story: the heartbreaking dilemma caused by a child's lack of friends, the importance of finding even one good friend, the value of sports and the arts or any other strong interest in creating a social life, and finally, the parents' (or grandparents') own sense of helplessness and sadness that sometimes seems greater than those experienced by the child. A mother whose teenage years were vibrant and filled with fun (or were uneventful, but pain-free) cannot help but compare her past to her child's present. A father who excelled at sports and has happy memories of team outings can be perplexed by his own son's inability to forge the same type of friendship, even if his child happens to be good at sports.

Let's talk about ways a parent can help.

Some of these behaviors or ways of thinking can be changed or, at least, improved. Some cannot. For instance, I can see no way to instill a sense of humor where none exists.

In order to help Allegra join in conversations, I always suggested she watch *The Today Show* so she would at least know the news of the day and read *People Magazine* for gossip about celebrities and new movies. (Teens today could read online news and entertainment sites, such as TMZ or People.com.)

Allegra also compliments people on what they are wearing, their appearance, or how nice they are. She has learned this is a good way to win over practically everyone. She does it online too: when she comments about a picture of a child or a pet or a grandparent, she will always write the same message: "Very special picture filled with love," followed by several heart emojis. It's very sweet and endears her to her online community.

Entire books can be written about ways to help with social skills, and in fact, many have. One in particular stands out. I highly recommend Rick Lavoie's book *It's So Much Work to Be Your Friend.* He wrote it in 2005 but the information is still extremely relevant and the advice will never go out of style.

One of Rick's most useful concepts is what he calls a social skills autopsy. As in a real autopsy when a pathologist tries to discover the cause of a person's death, a social skill autopsy is when a parent or teacher reviews a situation that has caused trouble to try to figure out what went wrong, and what can be done to prevent such difficulties in the future. As an example, you're standing in line at the grocery store ready to check out, and your thirteen year old daughter with LD points to the lady in line behind you and says, "What's wrong with her? Why does she wear her hair like that?" First, if you haven't died of embarrassment, I would have the daughter immediately apologize. There's no need to explain *why* at that moment – just apologize. I would then take her outside and go over the incident in detail in an attempt to get her to understand why that was very inappropriate, and try to turn it into a learning experience to prevent such things from happening in the future.

If your child is having trouble with social skills, the key to getting support is to discover the type of problems he or she is having and, if possible, find out why the problems arise. A good place to start is to observe your child in social situations and, like Matthew's grandmother, take detailed notes. These notes will be helpful to the professionals who evaluate him. Understanding your child's issues may be a multi-step process.

Here are some additional ideas adapted from information found on the invaluable website for the National Center for Learning Disabilities: *www.ncld.org*

- Talk to your child's teacher. You may have a good idea of your child's social difficulties at home, but the teacher can elaborate or provide new insights on what is happening in the classroom and on the playground. Sharing your concerns and observations can help the teacher put some informal support in place such as being sure to give clear instructions or assigning activities with other children who have similar interests.

- Consider an educational evaluation. If you suspect your child's social skills issues are caused by learning disabilities or ADHD, you (or your child's teacher) can request an evaluation. This, in turn, may lead to your child getting support and services. (For more information on getting evaluation services, I recommend my book *A Special Mother*, which goes into all of this in greater detail.)

- Talk to your child's pediatrician. If you discuss problems with social skills, the doctor may be able to rule out (or discover) any medical problems.

- Find a specialist. A psychologist trained in learning and attention issues can evaluate for non-verbal learning disabilities and ADHD, the two disorders that most often result in social problems. Also, a learning specialist can evaluate your child for learning and attention issues by using the same tests the school would use (though you will have to pay for this as it is a private evaluation.)

Whatever the cause may be of your child's troubles with social skills, you can help by getting support (both professional and personal), and taking actions to help improve social skills and building confidence. Children who have challenges with social skills do not usually outgrow them, but they certainly can learn strategies to help improve them. Success builds upon itself, and helps with self esteem and confidence, which, in turn, can lead to true and long-lasting friendships.

EPILOGUE

STIGMA DOES NOT HAVE TO WIN

One night, while talking to a friend, our conversation took an unexpected turn into distant, painful memories. "When I was in high school," she told me, "someone gave me a terrible nickname. I didn't know that's what people called me until I was walking across the playground one day and heard the name called out in a taunting way. I was the only one on the playground at the time and though I didn't see who called, I knew it was meant for me. I also knew that's what people called me behind my back because I heard it several times after that. I know it's crazy, but I think about that nickname all the time. I think about how it made me feel. Even now, I know it's like carrying baggage I no longer want but I can't seem to put down. I think I'll carry it for the rest of my life."

The woman who told me this was a vibrant, successful businesswoman in her fifties. She did not have LD. She did not have special needs or a disability of any kind. My point in telling this story is to show that *anyone* can suffer the effects of stigma, even if that stigma was experienced for only a short amount of time in the distant past. The effects can last for years and cause harmful effects long after the people who caused it have forgotten all about it.

When we add LD or related disorders to the mix, we can compound the stigma and the effects of stigma many times over.

What I've hoped to convey in this book is the reality that these things happen to nearly everyone. There is little chance of stopping it. I'm afraid it's human nature to look down on and disparage anyone who is "different". We can certainly *try* to stop it. We should try to stop it whenever possible, but the reality is that permanently changing this sort of ingrained human nature is nearly impossible. Rose-colored glasses sometimes show us the world as we believe it should be and not the world as it is. While that is admirable in its way, it does not always equip us for those times when something comes along to crack the lenses of those glasses.

What do we do in that case? How do we handle this unwelcome intrusion into our lives or the lives of our children?

I have tried in this book to cover the issues most associated with stigma: bullying, problems with social skills, how parents can overcome the stigma attached to LD, and most important, how to help your child do the same thing.

I assume anyone who has taken the trouble to read *The Stigmatized Child* already knows there is a problem, but if you are a parent who simply cannot get over the fact that your child has special needs, I have only this to say – you *must* get over it. There's no gentler way to put it. I can't help but wish someone had come along to say that to me. My denial was like living in a secret garden no one knew about but me. The walls kept me safe, or so I thought. I believed myself to be content and happy not answering questions. I thought it was nobody's business but my own. I did not realize I would have to interact with the world sooner or later, and no garden wall is high enough or strong enough to keep that world away.

How much different my life as a mother might have been if someone had come up to me and said, "Anne, this is the situation. Your daughter is exactly the same loving, fun, happy, joyful child she has always been and you have always known. She also happens to have a disability. She will not outgrow it. It will not go away. It will stay with her and affect her life and your life for the rest of your lives. The sooner you accept this and face it straight on, the easier things will be become – trust me."

It wasn't easy. It *still* isn't easy at times, but the fact remains: denial is a huge waste of time and can do actual damage if it means you don't seek out the help needed by your child (or you).

Talk it over with someone: a friend, a family member, a professional. Get help. Do not suffer in silence. Join (or start) a support group for other mothers. When I wrote my book *A Special Mother*, I interviewed a group of mothers in a small town in Massachusetts. Long after the book was published, they continued to meet once a month to talk about school and family issues. It was a chance to vent frustrations, to voice fears, and mostly, to see for themselves they were not alone in this.

For the child, stigma can be more devastating. Like my friend who carried the pain well into her fifties, the hurtful schoolyard taunts can outstay their welcome many times over. What do we do about this? As I said, it is a futile hope to think we can eradicate stigma from the world. Our best hope is to change our children's attitudes and ways of coping with it.

You are your child's most important ally in this. When the rest of the world is treating them badly or not taking them seriously, you must be there for them. That advice holds true for every mother and father, but for those whose children face the stigma of having special needs, it's even more important.

It all boils down to love and acceptance. I would go further and say it boils down to unconditional love…but not unconditional, or blind, acceptance.

Resilience is a vital and extremely useful life skill for children with learning and attention issues. Resilience helps children avoid being steam-rolled by adversity and allows them a little breathing room to learn coping skills and find ways to resolve challenges and difficulties. Facing these challenges straight on and learning lessons from them are beneficial. So is failure – *if* failure gives the child the chance to learn. Failure that only adds to low self-esteem is not useful (for instance, a child with dyscalculia who simply cannot add will probably not benefit from attempting, and failing, complicated algebra problems over and over and over.) But managed failure, or failure that leads to new understandings and positive outcomes, can be useful for everyone.

How do we teach resilience to a child who is fragile and unable to cope?

Underststood.org has created a list of helpful items to consider:

- Resist the urge to "fix" it. Sometimes our first inclination is to jump right in and make it right. A certain amount of amount of frustration isn't always a bad thing. It can lead to positive results, which can build persistence.

- Allow consequences to be the teacher. If your child does something that can lead to negative consequences, do not shield him or her from those consequences. Learning that an action taken can lead to an unwelcome consequence is one of life's most important lessons.

- Negative experiences can lead your child to find strategies that lead to positive outcomes. This again is what I call "managed failure". Mistakes that allow your child to see a way past it, through it, or around it, are valuable.

- Talk about lessons learned. Talk to your child about the strategies used and discuss things that could have been done differently and could have helped.

- Avoid a sink or swim situation. It's important to give your child enough support to face challenges, but not so much help that they can't make mistakes and learn from them.

- Expose your child to challenges. If your child doesn't have a chance to do things that are difficult, and perhaps fail at them, he or she will not have a chance to learn that particular lesson.

- Find every day situations where your child will need to work things out on their own. Do not be a helicopter parent, always nagging and second-guessing everything.

- Encourage your child to ask for additional support at school. He or she may not go through with this but will have the opportunity to learn how to persist in the face of a challenge and how to self-advocate.

Stigma is one of the meanest and most difficult aspects of having a child with any disability. You may not be able to change the way society feels overnight but we can help lessen the pain caused by stigma.

The answers are Resilience and Acceptance, and most of all, Love.

I end now with a vignette that inspired the subtitle of this book.

A mother was with her daughter in the park one sunny spring day last year. They had visited the Central Park zoo and ridden on the carousel. Something was bothering the daughter…the mother didn't know what it might be, but she was sure something was going on. The ten year old seemed preoccupied, but when asked, just shrugged her shoulders and said "nothing."

Near the end of the afternoon, they sat on a bench overlooking the reservoir and suddenly, without warning, the daughter turned to the mother and asked, simply: "Mommy, am I stupid?"

"The question was like a dagger to my heart," the mother told me. "I dissolved in tears though I tried not to show it." This was what had preoccupied her daughter. This was the secret she was carrying around, the idea that she was "stupid," and whether or not that idea was instilled by classmates, a schoolyard bully, a teacher or a family member, it found its mark and sank in and caused damage.

So what to do?

A simple, "of course not" and let the matter rest?

For some children, that might be all it would take.

Others may require a little more.

"You are not stupid," the mother told the daughter, "and whoever said that, doesn't know what they're talking about. You are in special education because you learn differently from others. It has nothing to do with whether or not you are smart. You are a wonderful sister to your little brothers. You love your cat Mittens and take such good care of her. You sing beautifully. You are a wonderful granddaughter, and you are the best daughter I could ever hope for. You have so many things in your life you do so well, and whenever you find something you don't do well, you know how to ask for help. That's the most important thing you can do."

This little speech encouraged her daughter and seemed to put her mind at rest. For the mother, it raised a flag – not a scary, red flag, but one that told her to be vigilant and aware that stigma might be on the prowl.

It also showed the mother that something can be done about it. Facing stigma head on and building up her child's confidence and abilities to handle whatever came her way were the answers.

Stigma may be an unavoidable part of the life of a child with disabilities, but as Dr. Horowitz said in his chapter, the good news is that stigma does not have to win.

About the Authors

Anne Ford served as Chairman of the Board of the National Center for Learning Disabilities (NCLD) from 1989 to 2001. During her term as Chair, she led the reorganization and broad expansion of NCLD, including establishing a presence in Washington, D.C., and organizing educational summits on learning disabilities in several regions of the United States. She has received many honors for her work in the field of learning disabilities, including the Lizette H. Sarnoff Award for Volunteer Service from the Albert Einstein College of Medicine. Leslie University has conferred upon her an Honorary Degree, Doctor of Humane Letters, for advocacy for people with learning disabilities. She is the author of the popular and inspirational book *Laughing Allegra* about her experiences as the mother of a daughter with learning disabilities; *On Their Own: Creating an Independent Future for Your Adult Child with Learning Disabilities and ADHD; A Special Mother: Getting Through the Early Days of a Child's Diagnosis of Learning Disabilities or Related Disorders;* and *The Forgotten Child: Sibling Issues: When Learning Disabilities Cause Tension in the Home.* She continues to work on behalf of people with LD, appearing as a speaker at conferences and corporations and schools.

John-Richard Thompson is an award-winning playwright and novelist living in New York City. He is co-author with Anne Ford of five books on learning disabilities. For more information, visit his website www.j-rt.com

For more visit:

www.anneford.net

Acknowledgements

We would like to thank all the many parents, young adults, and professionals who helped us with this book. Their honesty, compassion and advocacy formed the heart of our story. I feel that sometimes it was really quite painful for them to share their stories – in fact, I *know* it was. I heard it in their voices and saw it in their eyes. Their distress when talking about their child's isolation was at times overwhelming, but in agreeing to tell their stories, they have helped so many others experiencing similar problems.

We are so grateful to the mothers at the Gateway School and the Craig School. In addition, we would like to thank Dana Buchman and Charlotte Farber, Dr. Bob Cunningham, Dr. Cecelia Dintino, Casey Dixon, Donna Eichenwald, Susan Gabert, Dr. Sheldon Horowitz, Shelley Mosley-Stanzel, and Natalie Tamburello. I would also like to thank Dr. Jeffrey Lieberman and Glenn Close for taking the time out of their very busy schedules to offer their expertise.

We especially want to thank our agent Susan Cohen who has inspired and guided us from the very beginning. She has not only been our agent, but has been a true friend and a believer in all our books, from our very first one, *Laughing Allegra* through our fifth one, *The Stigmatized Child*.

I send much love and thanks to my daughter Allegra and my son Alessandro for their constant support, and my granddaughters Eleanor and Olivia.

Finally we thank you, the reader of this and all our books. You are the reason we do this. Your courage and efforts and efforts to advocate for your children are an inspiration to us all.